WISEWOMAN LEADERSHIP: Your Key to Leading with Ease, Grace and Integrity
Copyright © Kinnexion, LLC. All rights reserved.

These materials contain proprietary content and must not be duplicated, excerpted or distributed without written permission. No portion of these materials may be shared or reproduced in any manner under any circumstance whatsoever without advance written permission.
Contact for Reuse and Distribution Requests:

Kinnexion LLC
3231 Kingswood Dr.
Sarasota, FL 34232
jbarr@kinnexion.com

Editor: Susan Hicks

Published by Kinnexion LLC
3231 Kingswood Dr.
Sarasota, FL 34232
jbarr@kinnexion.com

Cover and Book Design: White Studios

ISBN 978-0-9996658-0-0

Table of Contents

Dedication	5
Executive Summary	6
Introduction – From SuperWoman to WiseWoman	9

Step 1 – Take Control of Your Success
1. Mid-Career Magic — 17
2. Stumbling Blocks — 27
3. Your Magic Formula — 39

Step 2 – Choose Your Perspective
4. First Steps Toward WiseWoman Leadership — 57
5. Fighting Your Way to the Top — 75
6. Living in the Yin and the Yang — 91

Step 3 – WiseWoman Leadership
7. Opportunity Knocks — 107
8. Comparing Different Leadership Approaches — 125
9. Beyond the Ordinary — 139

The Feminine Advantage
10. A New Perspective — 157

Dedication

This book is dedicated to all the smart, strong, savvy women working in the field of technology. Thank you for your contributions and for your courage and tenacity, which have allowed you to thrive in this very male-dominated field and to be examples of strength to women everywhere.

Executive Summary

Introduction

From SuperWoman to WiseWoman — 9
Women hate the label "SuperWoman," because the expectation is that we have to 'do it all' to be successful. What if we changed our label to "WiseWoman"?

Step 1 – Take Control of Your Success

1. Mid-Career Magic — 17
You love your work and are successful, yet something isn't working quite right because it often feels like a struggle. What key opens the door to working with ease, grace and integrity?

2. Stumbling Blocks — 27
If we knew what caused us to stress, struggle or become overwhelmed, we would have already stopped. What do we need to know about how the brain works that will allow us to shift our experience?

3. Your Magic Formula — 39
When life gets easier, it can feel magical. How do we shift our work experience without having to constantly pay attention to our every behavior or every word we say and respond to situations authentically?

Step 2 – Choose Your Perspective

4. First Steps Toward WiseWoman Leadership — 57
Stress is the number one cause of dis-ease. What is the primary reason for stress in the workplace, and what do we need to change to reduce stress?

5. Fighting Your Way to the Top   75
Most people will tell you that in order to be successful, they had to struggle or fight their way to the top. But is that the best way and if not, what might be a better answer?

6. Living in the Yin and Yang   91
Yin and Yang, masculine and feminine – there are different ways of looking at work. How do the differences affect us, and is it really necessary to take on a masculine role to succeed?

Step 3 – WiseWoman Leadership

7. Opportunity Knocks   107
Men and women think and act differently. Where is the opportunity that allows us to respect and honor both approaches and at the same time create a more productive work environment?

8. Comparing Different Leadership Approaches   125
Taking several real-life work situations we compare the effect of using five different leadership approaches. Which one works best for you, and what would you change to make your life easier?

9. Beyond the Ordinary   139
An athlete at the top of their game talks about being in the flow. Great scientists are known for their genius ideas. What is it that takes a leader a step or two beyond the ordinary to extraordinary?

The Feminine Advantage

10 A New Perspective   157
Women have an advantage (yes, an advantage) in the workplace that most of us have not tapped into. How can you use your feminine advantage and lead us into a new chapter in business success?

WISEWOMAN LEADERSHIP

Introduction

From SuperWoman to WiseWoman Leadership

Are you as sick of the label 'SuperWoman' as I am? When I started my coaching business, I decided that the woman I was trying to reach out to and support was embodied in the image of 'SuperWoman.' I wanted to work with high power women, women who were going places and making fantastic contributions to their organizations, their communities and the world. Here is how I described my ideal client: She is the woman with a successful career in technology that she loves. She is a respected leader. She is caring, compassionate and highly involved with her family and friends. She volunteers in her community. She takes good care of herself and has a strong physical presence. And she makes it all look so easy.

Another coach and I even planned out a retreat for SuperWomen called P.O.W., which stood for Power of Women. We had posters drawn up of a woman in a business suit zooming down the street in her hot sports car with a cape blowing out the back window and cartoon balloons above her with words like "POW," "BAM" and "WOW." You get the picture. When I look back on it, I cringe at the narrow way in which we were thinking about women and work.

The good thing is that in the process of developing this marketing message, I decided to put out a request for feedback on social media. A wonderful woman, Jessica Rivelli, who has a women's networking group with 800+ members called Working Women of Tampa Bay, picked up my request and shared it with her group. There was a ton of feedback (thank you), and the overwhelming response was *I hate the label 'SuperWoman'!!!*

What I heard was that even though women want to be successful in their own right, they are sick and tired of being sick and tired. Women are tired of working twice as hard as a man in order to be promoted into leadership. Women are tired of making less money than men for the same work. Women are tired of being expected to not only work long hours, but also take care of family matters, whether that is children, aging parents or just being responsible for dinner every night. Women are tired of having their ideas ignored, rejected or stolen by a man. Women are tired of being judged by how they look and not by their intelligence or what ideas and value they contribute. They are tired of saying something the same way a man would say it and being criticized for it. I could go on and on, but the bottom line is that women are tired of trying to be SuperWoman, and they want something better.

Here's what I believe and have experienced regarding this situation. We can solve most of our concerns right here and now, simply by learning to think differently. We can be rewarded for our contributions, have financial security, be respected for our intelligence and what we contribute, have a greater sense of freedom, feel fulfilled and truly enjoy our work, and have more of whatever else we want, simply by changing our perspective.

To be honest, I think that innately you know this is true. You know that how you look at a situation can make a big difference. On the other hand, you may ask, if it's that simple, why am I so exhausted all the time? Why, after all my hard work, am I still feeling insecure about my financial future? Why do I have to do it all by myself in order to be successful?

It may simply be that no one has ever taken the time to sit down with you and share with you exactly how to think differently in order to make your life better. Someone may have said to you, "Just think positively" or "Put on a happy face and life will be better." No doubt you may have thought, "Right, as if you really understand what I am going through or the situation that I'm in right now or the people I have to deal with every day."

In my experience, slapping a happy face on everything or finding the good in a bad situation or making lemonade out of lemons are great band aids, but they don't cure the hurt. Hurt, whether physical, mental or emotional, has to be cured from the inside out. We have to learn to think differently in order to experience different results.

The answer is also not a series of behavior modification techniques that work in one situation but not necessarily in another, and that we have to constantly pay attention to in order to work. Most women are already on overload. We don't need to add behavior 'to does' to our plates.

And perhaps most important, we don't need to change who we are or act like a man in order to be successful. Hiding who we are as a woman or acting in a particular way (i.e., like a man) in order to be successful can actually backfire on us. When we try to act a certain way in order to fit into a culture, not only is it uncomfortable for us, the effect is like putting on a mask. People don't know who is behind the mask, and there can be a sense that we can't be trusted.

Instead of trying to be something that we are not, what I propose is that we allow ourselves to be the phenomenal women that we are, to authentically step forward and be fully recognized for the value that we bring to the table as women, and to do that with ease, grace and integrity.

From SuperWoman to WiseWoman

OK, Jane, so you seem to "know it all." (Insert eye roll here.) How are we going to do that? Over the past 10 years, I have developed a coaching program I call WiseWoman Leadership. My definition of a WiseWoman is a woman who has the ability to be in the flow, like an athlete at the top of her game, while at the same time gaining the respect and recognition she deserves, having a feeling of accomplishment and impact on the world, and having a sense of freedom about her career and finances.

In my personal experience and in coaching women in leadership roles, I have found that it takes three distinct steps to become WiseWoman Leaders.

The first step is to become aware of what we can and cannot change. In my experience, it is a lot easier to change what is going on in our own head than it is to try and change someone else. Becoming aware of our thoughts, emotions, actions and how they are affecting our results is the magical first step in our success story. I refer to this step as: Taking Control of Your Success.

The second step is learning how to shift our thoughts, emotions and actions in a specific pattern that allows us to actually achieve what we intend while remaining true to who we are as women. It's great to be aware of our thoughts, but if we don't understand how our thoughts correlate to our results, we may find ourselves in control and succeeding on the outside but suffering from overwork, stress and frustration on the inside. It is interesting that this step has helped both women and men to be successful in their careers.

The final step I refer to as being in the flow or WiseWoman Leadership. It's one thing to have the career you want, to be financially stable, and to be seen by the world as successful. It is quite another thing to be able to do that with ease, grace and integrity, and a complete sense of freedom. What would it be like if you could have work that satisfied you at the deepest level of your soul? What would it be like if you felt totally financially free? What would it be like to feel fulfilled and find lasting joy in your work? What would it be like to do all this as the most authentic and natural you?

I know that you have within you the power to be, do and have everything that you truly want in your life. I truly believe that, with a better understanding of the power that we hold as women, we can all learn to be WiseWoman Leaders.

In truth, the simple fact that you are taking the time to read this book tells me that you already are a WiseWoman Leader, even if you don't recognize it in yourself right now. You already hold the key to a different way of living and leading.

It is my vision to share what I have learned with as many women as possible, so that we can all be valued and recognized for our full potential, have careers and personal lives that not only look successful on the outside but also satisfy us on the inside, and experience all of this with a sense of ease, grace and integrity.

My hope is that as you read through this book, experience some of the exercises and integrate the concepts of WiseWoman Leadership into your life, that you will start to see a shift in your career and that your whole life will become happier and more fulfilling and successful, whatever success may mean to you.

Step 1

Take Control of Your Success

Chapter 1

Mid-Career Magic

You might think that with 20+ years of experience as a consultant to national retailers such as GAP, CVS and REI, I would have perfected the art and science of business. But little did I know just how much I was missing until I ran into a nasty bump in the road.

It's August 2006. I'm about 6 months into a consulting project with an international handbag manufacturer and retailer. With my background and experience, I could have been leading the project. Instead, I'm sitting in the team room creating flow charts. This is the type of work I was doing when I started my career. I know the flow charts are important to the project, but truthfully...I'm not very excited about doing the work.

This particular day the project manager walks over to my desk and tells me that we are getting a new technical resource on the team.

I say, "Great. When is this person arriving?"

He says, "She's arriving today and.........I want her to take your desk and........I want you to take your work and move to the office back in the warehouse."

Ugh!

It's a long walk back to the office in the warehouse. As I move through the front office, then the cafeteria, then the hallway into the warehouse, my head starts to pound. This is not good. I was already feeling somewhat disconnected from the team because of what I perceived to be an age gap. For the first time in my career, I am the oldest person on the team by at least 10 years, including the project leader. This move isn't going to make the situation any better.

As I walk through the cafeteria, I hear people laughing and it triggers a thought. I remember that the only other person working in the warehouse office is the person that the team has been making fun of for months. I ask myself, "What does that say about me? Am I laughable?"

As I'm walking, fear starts to build up in my mind that I might lose my job. My husband and I spent the last 4 years building a business which used up a big chunk of our savings. In addition, our son is in college and, as anyone knows who has a child in college, it's not cheap. Quite frankly, I need this job, possibly more than it needs me.

By the time I get to the hallway that leads to the warehouse office, my fear turns into anger. My pace has quickened and I'm practically stomping my way down that hallway. To be truthful, I'm not sure if I am more angry at the project manager (and yes, the thought did go through my head that he was just another male jerk) for asking me to move or at myself, for getting into this situation in the first place. The thing is, I have led projects like this in the past, actually much larger projects than this one, and I know in my gut that I have the experience, the knowledge and the character to be leading this project. Yet, where am I? I'm on my way to an office in the warehouse to create more flow charts.

As I reach the door to the office in the warehouse, I stop and I make a firm decision. I am NOT going to spend the rest of my career in an office in a warehouse creating flow charts. This very firm decision is the beginning of my search for answers to why, as much as I love my career, it feels to me that I am like a bird locked in a golden cage, trapped by the pay I need to support my family, feeling frustrated with the direction my work has gone in the last year, tired from the load of work that is piling up and fearful that I may be in danger of getting the boot.

In my searching for answers, what I discover is that I'm holding the key to my cage. The key is a concept called *Radical Personal Responsibility*. Without a doubt, this is the most powerful concept I have learned, and it very quickly starts to change my entire world. Within three short months of grasping the concept of *Radical Personal Responsibility*, my career takes a dramatic turn. I am asked to participate as a speaker on a national tour for the very same client where three months earlier I had been asked to move to the office back in the warehouse. On my next project, I'm put in charge of a section for the complete re-engineering of all systems for another national retailer. Two years later, I'm hired to lead a project for a third national retailer at almost twice my former pay. How did this all happen so quickly? The answer starts with understanding the concept of *Radical Personal Responsibility*.

Let me stop here for a minute and tell you straightforward that I am not sharing what happened to me in order to brag. I'm telling you about my results from using this concept in order to inspire you to want to use it as well. In truth, anyone who is reading this book has the ability to easily learn and then put this concept to use in their own lives. And when you fully integrate this concept into your life, you will have control of your success.

What is Radical Personal Responsibility?

When most people think about responsibility, they think in terms of showing up on time, following through with a promise, or meeting a deadline. True?

But what happens if we take responsibility and something goes wrong? We may not always take responsibility for that situation. Sometimes we blame the circumstances, sometimes we blame other people, and sometimes we blame God or the Universe for our situation. And yes, sometimes we blame ourselves.

The problem with blaming circumstances, people, a deity or

even ourselves for our problem, is that then the situation is out of our control. If the situation is out of our control, then there is nothing we can do about it. We are DOOMED.

Some of you may be thinking – but isn't blaming ourselves the same as taking responsibility? Not really. Blaming causes us to feel guilty or not good enough. It takes away our power. When we blame ourselves, we may subconsciously give our self an excuse for not taking action. On the other hand, when we take responsibility for a situation, the sense is that there is something that we can and will do to change the situation.

Radical Personal Responsibility is taking personal responsibility for everything that is happening in our lives. Yes, I said everything.

OK, I can almost hear you saying, "Wait just a minute. Are you saying that I am responsible for the world economy or the weather? That's just crazy talk!"

Essentially, you are right. It's crazy to think that as an individual we can control something like the weather. And blaming ourselves or being hard on ourselves doesn't make a situation better either. However, what we can do is take responsibility for how we respond to any situation, including the weather. When we take radical personal responsibility for how we respond to any given situation, it figuratively and literally changes our reality.

For example, I'm sure you have seen different people react to the same storm a myriad of ways. One person reacts to a storm as being a big nuisance, coming into work without a raincoat or umbrella, the whole time complaining about getting wet. I'm sure we have all had to put up with a complainer in our office. Another person finds the storm to be a source of scientific fascination. They take out their rain and wind gauges to track the changes in the storm. All day they look out the window and point out unusual cloud formations. And still others, like many children, look at a storm as one giant puddle inviting them to come outside and play. It is one storm and three very different responses to that same storm. Each reaction creates a different reality for the individual person and affects the people around them.

These are not the only reactions people have to the weather. There are literally thousands of ways of reacting. The concern here is not that we have different reactions. Having different reactions to any situation or person is normal and natural. The concern is that we think that how we are reacting is just the way things are, that we have no control over how we respond to a situation.

When something isn't working for us, our tendency may be to say, "Well, it's raining and there is nothing I can do about it. I guess I'll just hunker down and wait it out." When things are working for us, we may say, "What a beautiful rain. It will be great to see all the plants revive from the water." We totally miss the point that we are looking at the same rain from two points of view and…that we have control over how we view the rain and how we let it affect our day.

The same can be said for any situation or relationship. It is not the situation or person which is the determining factor in how our day goes or for that matter in how successful we are in our careers. The determining factor is our perspective on the situation. *Radical Personal Responsibility* means becoming acutely aware of our thoughts or perspective on a given situation, and then, if a situation isn't working for us, shifting our thoughts which in turn shifts our reality.

Let's look at an example in the workplace that will hopefully make this clearer for you. My client Debbie (not her real name) is a recruiter for engineering firms. A few years ago, during a recession, she was downsized. She decided to pick up some contracting work to make ends meet until she found another full-time job. She was doing fairly well with her contracting, starting out with some small jobs before she landed a contract that would keep her busy for at least six months.

One day she called me in a near panic. She had already finished more than half of the recruiting work on this large contract and she still had not received a check for any of her work. Not only was she not getting paid, but her contact at the company was not returning her calls. She was scared, and understandably so. This was her livelihood.

I asked her what she thought was going on. She said, "I'm afraid they are using me and that he is avoiding me so he doesn't have to pay me. If this continues, I won't have enough money to pay my bills. And what if he doesn't give me a good referral? I could lose out on future contracts or not be able to land a full-time job."

And then she said some things which signaled to me that she was ready to take *Radical Personal Responsibility* for the situation. She asked, "Why does this always happen to me?" and "What am I going to do?" and finally, "I have to find a way to turn this around!" In other words, at that very moment she made a decision to take control of her success.

At that point, I asked her what other reasons her contact might have for not calling her. And she said, "I don't know." Again, her response was very normal. When we are in the heat of the moment or if we have experienced a similar situation in the past, we may unconsciously limit how we look at a situation.

I suggested that we brainstorm some other possible scenarios other than the one she was picturing in her mind. We came up with five possibilities.

1. Maybe he put in the requisition for her check and then had to leave on an assignment and wasn't there to make sure her check was cut, signed and mailed.

2. Maybe he is avoiding her because he is really bad at organization and is feeling uncomfortable about not giving her paperwork to accounting as yet.

3. Maybe he is sick and doesn't realize that his assistant didn't take care of the paperwork.

4. Maybe there is a person above him that has to sign off on the paperwork. Every time she calls her contact, it is a reminder to him that his boss doesn't respect him enough to take care of these details.

5. Maybe he was run over by a Mac truck. – Yuck.

After we finished brainstorming, I asked her which one was true, and she said, "I have no idea."
Then I asked her how she could find out. She decided that the easiest thing to do was to call a couple of people she knew in the company and ask if they had seen or talked with her contact recently.
The next day Debbie called me back. She said, "You are not going to believe this, but he was in an accident and is in the hospital. I feel bad about the negative messages I left on his voice mail. I wish I could go in and erase them. I bought a funny card and took it to him at the hospital. He was all apologetic and told me who to talk with about getting paid. I am so relieved."
Immediately upon discovering the truth, Deb's thoughts about the situation changed. She shifted from thinking that she was not going to get paid and that she was going to fail, to thinking that everything was going to work out fine for her. At the same time, her feelings shifted. She went from feeling anxious and near pan-

icked to feeling relieved and even a bit chagrined about her initial reactions to the situation. And not only did her thoughts and feelings change, but her results changed. She got her paycheck!

Note that nothing changed until Deb changed her thoughts. As soon as she took *Radical Personal Responsibility* for the situation, she was able to shift her thoughts and feelings and to create a different reality for herself.

Some of you may be saying to yourself, "Well, that's all fine and good that her contact turned out to actually respect her work and was willing to pay her. But what if you were in a situation where your client really doesn't want to pay you?"

Another client, I'll call her Lauren, came to me with that exact concern. She told me that her boss had a family friend that he wanted to help out. The friend had a small business, and Lauren's boss offered to have his company create a website for it. The plan had been to create a very simple, straightforward website that wouldn't cost a lot of money. The problem was that as the project moved along, the client kept wanting more and more changes and more web pages. When they discussed the fact that the price they had quoted her was for a specific number of pages and that the additional pages would cost more money, she became angry. She took what she had and went to another website designer who added the pages. And she didn't pay my clients' company. Instead she used her money to pay the second designer.

For weeks, my client had been wrestling with the situation. A couple times she had gingerly attempted a conversation with the client but had received the cold shoulder. My client knew this was a family friend of her boss and she didn't want to create more of a conflict than had already occurred, which made her hesitant to continue to ask for their payment. At the same time, they had subcontractors who had completed some of the work and they needed to be paid. This was putting them in the hole financially on this project.

When I asked her what would have to happen to make this a good situation, she said, "I wish the situation could just disappear."

At that point, I knew she had made a decision and was ready to think differently. I asked her how she thought her boss would react if she suggested that they do exactly what she wanted to do, i.e. simply stop going after the money and pay the contractors using money from another project.

She hesitated for a minute and then said that she thought he would actually be relieved, especially if she could find a way for him to save face, since it was his idea to take on the project, and if she could recommend another way to pay the subcontractors.

As we talked through the situation, we discovered that they did not have a thorough enough process for detailing the project expectations and getting signoff from the client before going into the development stage.

Lauren took the time to create a more detailed process. Then she went to her boss and told him that as a company they had made a mistake in not taking his friend through a thorough enough planning process, and she recommended that they drop the charges and use this experience as a lesson and inspiration for developing a better process. She also had a recommendation for how to pay the subcontractors. Then she presented him with her suggestions for a new process.

Lauren told me that her boss quickly agreed to drop the charges and move on.

Another good thing came out of this situation. They were in the beginning stages of a similar project, and this new project was much bigger. Because of what they learned from the smaller project, they had a much better planning process that helped them not only to stay on track but also to have a more professional relationship with their client.

Isn't it amazing what happens when we are willing to take *Radical Personal Responsibility* for a situation? Situations that seem like huge problems suddenly become an opportunity to make our life easier. Simply stated: The more we take *Radical Personal Responsibility* for what is happening in our lives, the more we are in control of our success.

Chapter 2

Stumbling Blocks

One question that may be coming up for you right now is: "If it's so easy to shift our thoughts, then what is keeping me from discovering what is going on in my mind and changing it, so that I can take control of my success?" To understand what is going on, it may help to know a little bit about how the brain works.

Stop reading for a minute and look around you. Notice all of the colors and shapes you see in the room where you are right now. What do you see? What do you hear? What do you smell?

Do you know that scientists tell us that our brain takes in roughly four billion bits of information every second? And did you know that 99.99999 percent of that brain activity is happening in our subconscious, where we are unaware of what is happening?

By comparison, our conscious brain activity, which takes place in the frontal cortex, can only process about forty thousand bits of information every second. In other words, there is a huge gap between what our brain can subconsciously process (4 billion bits) and what it is consciously processing (40,000 bits).

What if our brain tried to consciously process all 4 billion bits of information at one time? It would probably explode!

This is where our subconscious comes in. Our subconscious builds patterns that it uses to filter information, so we don't have to consciously think about everything. It is very similar to a computer application that is programmed to recognize certain bits of information and process them automatically in the background without any human intervention.

How do the patterns get formed?

Let's consider a visual pattern first. Say, for example, that when you were a child someone pointed out an object to you and said, "This is a chair." And then they pointed out a similar object and called it a chair. Maybe you had a book with a picture of a chair and each time someone read that book to you they pointed out the chair. This continued until eventually you recognized what a chair was without having to consciously think about it. Now when you walk into a room, you don't look at all the objects in a room and wonder which one is the chair. You know what a chair is and you automatically, without consciously thinking about it, go to the chair and sit down.

The same thing happens with all of our mental and emotional thought patterns as well. We create patterns of thought that our brain uses to filter information, so it doesn't have to process all of the information at the conscious level.

Here is an example of what I mean by patterns of thought that we create. I was probably 4 or 5 years old. My family was in Arkansas at an uncle's home in the country. Across a field was another relative's home. That relative had a small black-and-white television. When I was growing up, the people I was normally around didn't own televisions, and I had never heard of or seen a television.

My older brother and a cousin decided to go across the field to see the television. They sounded very excited and I wanted to go as well. My older brother said something to the affect that I couldn't go because I was a girl and I was too little. My mother agreed. And then the boys left to see the television.

That did not sit very well with me! Even as a very young child, I was up for adventure and new discoveries, and the excitement in my brother's voice told me that this was something not to be missed. As soon as my mother's back was turned and she was involved in another conversation, I took off across that field after my brother and cousin. I was determined to see this thing called a television.

Being very small, the weeds in the field were way over my head and there were bees buzzing all around me. It was very scary, but I pushed my way past those bees and on to the other house. I felt very alone on this big adventure (and was not aware that my parents were watching to make sure I was safe).

Happily, I got to see the television with the sound and moving pictures! It was so fascinating. I loved it.

At that moment, a thought pattern was formed in my head. The pattern informed me that if I wanted to do and see things that were exciting, I would have to go against what the big guys said, turn my back on my mother and father, go out on my own, not expect or ask for help, and fight past tall weeds and scary bees.

To protect my brain from having to think about similar situations, I unconsciously started looking for similar patterns in my life. For example, when I was eight I insisted on going to a camp without my older brother. When I was 10, I learned to shoot a gun and beat all the boys at marksmanship, even though I was told I was too small to hold the gun. When I was 11, I learned to sail and play "chicken on the lake" and managed to tip over a boat full of boys. If I think about it, I could probably come up with dozens of other examples.

That pattern was so set in my subconscious that until I was in my early 40s, I subconsciously believed that in order to have what I really wanted in my life, I had to turn my back on my mother and father, and I had to go up against the big guys and be aggressive in my actions. I had to fight to get what I wanted in my life.

To some extent that helped me move ahead in my career, because I wouldn't take 'No' for an answer. On the other hand, it often made my life difficult, because people perceived me to be stubborn and defensive and not particularly likeable. It wasn't until someone pointed out that there was another way to think about how to reach my goals that I started to behave differently.

The interesting thing is that I didn't realize that it was a subconscious pattern. I simply thought that the world was difficult for women and we had no choice but to fight to get ahead in business.

Creating a pattern in my brain isn't something that happened just to me. It happens to everyone all the time. It's how our brains operate. For instance, maybe someone told you that because you didn't brush your teeth, you were bad. Your brain wanted to create a pattern of "bad," so it wouldn't have to consciously process that thought again. In this instance, your brain might have looked for other times when you were labeled as "bad" for not doing something. Maybe you made a mistake on a spelling test and the teacher put a big red -3 on your paper and someone said that it was a "bad" mistake. Because you made the error, you associated that label "bad" with yourself. Or perhaps you were learning a sport like swimming and your body wasn't strong enough or you were tired during training and the coach said that you were 'bad' at what you were doing. After a while you created a filter in your subconscious mind that you were bad or perhaps not good enough. That thought became submerged in your subconscious and you started to associate that thought with yourself, as though that thought was your very being. For you, it seemed true. You were bad. And you subconsciously carried that label into adulthood.

The problem is that as long as we don't challenge that thought pattern, it will continue on and we will view our world through the filter of "I'm bad" or "I'm not good enough." Those thoughts may very well be preventing us from doing what we would like to do so that we can have what we want in our life.

But the truth is that our thoughts are just that…they are thoughts, nothing more. Our thoughts are not who we are, and we can change our thoughts and change our reality. Just like the example in the first chapter relative to what happens when we encounter a storm, we can decide how we want to think about the storm, and the storm can either be our enemy or become our friend.

Although the majority of our thought patterns are formed when we are very young, we continue to develop patterns throughout our life based on what we learn through our experiences, information we gather through various tools such as books or media, and ideas we receive from other people.

Consider this scenario. You just found a new place to live. The first few times you go there, maybe you follow a map or your GPS. Then it starts to get a little more familiar and you carefully watch for street signs and turns. After a while the way home becomes so familiar that you don't have to think about it. One day you find yourself in your driveway and you realize…you don't know how you got there. Guess what, your brain has created a pattern and your subconscious has taken over.

Your brain created this pattern so you wouldn't have to consciously think about the drive home. It freed up your conscious brain to think about other things. On your way home, you probably were thinking about what to make for dinner or a conversation at work that didn't go how you had hoped it would or the wonderful person you met that day.

That sounds productive, doesn't it? But did you know that most accidents happen within three miles of our home? Our brains tend to go on autopilot, and we don't notice when something is happening that varies from our normal pattern. And what happens when someone unexpectedly cuts in front of us? If we are on autopilot, an accident is likely to happen.

Just like the pattern that was formed to allow us to drive home on autopilot, all of our thought patterns were established initially to allow our brain to function efficiently. The concern isn't that our brain creates patterns. The concern is: We aren't aware of these patterns. When the world changes around us and we are on autopilot, not aware of our thought patterns, then life can become difficult, simply because our thought patterns don't work for us in the current situation.

The good news is that, just like my clients, we can become aware of our thought patterns and change them so that they better serve us. Here's an example of how we can learn a thought pattern even as an adult that can make our life difficult, and how a simple change in thought can radically change our life.

My client, whom I'll call Sara, told me that she was concerned about her company. I could hear the stress in her voice. Sara previously had been a vice president for an international technology services company. About 7 years before our conversation, she had stepped out and started her own consulting company. Her company had a lot of success in a certain area of work. But now those types of projects were winding down, and she didn't know in what direction to take her company next.

I asked her what she was doing to figure out her next direction. She said that what she needed to do first was read a number of industry magazines and listen to webinars so that she could start to get a handle on business trends. Next, she needed to consider her company's expertise. When she had all of this information, she would be able to decide on an area of consulting that would be on trend, match her company's expertise, and be valuable to potential clients. However, she was so overwhelmed with her day-to-day workload that she didn't have time for reading or listening to webinars.

She told me that every night she was putting all of her reading materials in her briefcase and carrying them home with her. But when she got home, she was so tired that they never came out of the briefcase. She had dinner, played a few video games and went to bed. The next morning, she carried the reading materials back to work with her. She had been carrying those magazines back and forth, day in and day out for months on end. Has anyone else ever done something similar? Me too!

We talked about a few other ways she might find time to read, such as shutting her office door for an hour several times a week. She insisted that she could not close her door and that her employees and clients had to have access to her at all times during the workday in order to keep projects on track. She had a strict open-door policy in the office.

We talked about handing over the research on trends to another person in the company. She didn't feel that there was anyone else in the company who had her level of knowledge and experience. In addition, as the owner of the company, she felt she needed to do this strategy work herself.

After a few more ideas were tossed around it occurred to me to ask her, "Who told you that you can't close your door?"

She was very quiet for a couple of minutes. In fact, so quiet that I questioned if she was OK. All of a sudden she practically shouted into the phone, "It was my first boss and I didn't even like him. He used to walk around and if we were in our cubicle reading an industry magazine or even a contract, he would point his finger at us and say, 'Stop reading and put that away right now. Reading is for your off hours. When you are in the office, you are to be working on current projects with your colleagues and clients.'"

As soon as Sara recognized that it was her thoughts that were getting in her way, she immediately shifted into thinking that it was OK for her to shut her office door and take time to work on her business strategy. At the same time, her feelings of being overwhelmed shifted and she became calmer. She chuckled and asked to stop for a minute so she could book a couple of hours into her week to close her door and read. And she is still doing that today. The result is that she is happier and her business is healthier.

Hopefully by now you are noticing the commonality between these examples of *Radical Personal Responsibility*. The commonality is this: When you change your thoughts, your thoughts automatically shift your emotions. Your shift in emotions drives different actions, and because of these changes, the world responds differently to you, and then your reality changes.

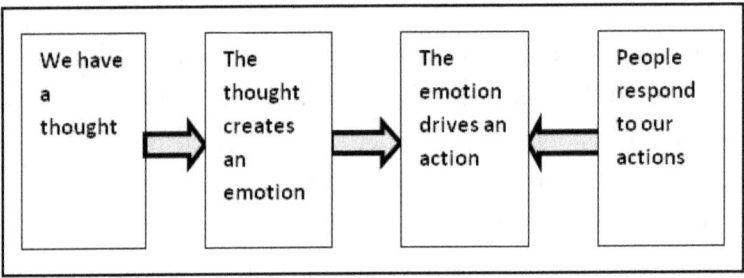

Notice also that people cannot see what we are thinking or feeling. What other people experience is our actions, and it is our actions that people respond to. When we shift our thoughts, we feel differently and act differently. The result is that people experience us differently and respond back to us in a new way.

You are a smart person and you know instinctively that you cannot change another person. How many of you have ever tried to change your partner? Next to impossible, isn't it? If you think about it relative to how the mind works, it makes sense. Everyone is doing the exact same thing you are doing, filtering the world through their own patterns or filters. They aren't in your head and you aren't in their head. The only person that can change your mind is you, and the only person that can change another person's mind is the other person.

On the other hand, we deserve to be treated with respect and valued for our contributions. So how do we effectively change how people treat us? How do we influence a situation? How do we create our world? *We do it first by shifting our thoughts, which shifts our emotions, which shifts our actions, which shifts the way people respond to us.*

How might this work for you? To recognize it for yourself, let's start with a simple exercise called "Choosing Our Words."

Choosing Our Words

Every day we have to make choices. Yet many of us walk around feeling that we have limited choices in many aspects of our lives. In fact, when we're faced with a task or something to do, there are many ways we can choose to respond. Let's discover right now what it might feel like to take *Radical Personal Responsibility* with our words.

Exercise:

1. Take out a piece of paper or better yet find a partner.

2. Write and/or say out loud: "I _____ go to work.

3. Fill in the blank (one at a time) with the words: can't, have to, should, need to, choose to, get to, and love to.

4. As you read the sentence out loud with each of the different

words, pay attention to how you feel when you say each of the sentences.

5. If you have a partner, ask them to notice your facial expressions, tone of voice and body language as you use each word.

6. What have you discovered? Are there certain sentences that make you feel stressed, frustrated, in control, calm, joyful, inspired?

Notice that each of these words is associated with a different thought, feeling and action. What do you think would happen if you became aware of your thinking? What if, when you thought the word "should," you consciously changed it to "want"? Would you feel different? Would you act differently? How do you think people would respond to your different actions?

Here is how some people have interpreted each of these words. See if these interpretations ring true for you.

1. "I can't" - When we say "I can't," we believe that we do not have a choice, or we think that taking action will not result in positive results for us – so, why do it? Or we may believe that it is out of our control to be able to change a situation, and because we believe we can't do anything to affect the outcome, we avoid taking action.

2. "I have to" - If we say "I have to," we feel forced to complete the task in front of us or else we will experience negative consequences. We don't see a choice, even when it's right in front of us. That can trigger feelings of fear, frustration, anger or resentment.

3. "I should" - One of my favorite reminders is, "Don't 'should' on yourself." When we say "I should," we are generally following subconscious rules that we learned as children or young adults, whether or not they benefit us as adults. If a rule no longer serves us, yet we believe "I should" follow the rule, it can create a sense of overwhelm. If we don't follow an "I should," then we may feel guilty. Either way there is stress.

4. "I need to" - This perspective brings more chance of success *if* we are aware that we have choices and shift from **"I need to"** to **"I can,"** and then determine a strategy to meet our challenges. However, if our thoughts shift from **"I need to"** resolve this situation to **"I can't"** resolve this situation, then we can be left feeling needy or focused on what is lacking in a situation. When we are focused on lack, it is next to impossible to see opportunities, even if they are right in front of us.

5. "I want to" - This response indicates that we are mostly at choice. We may want something, we may know we have a choice, but we don't always make the choice that will allow us to live the life we want.

6. "I choose to" - When we respond this way, we feel we have complete choice. There's a powerful connection between who we are and what we do, and we can feel a rise in energy from choice.

7. "I get to" - Try taking a situation where you use one of the phrases above and just see how different you feel if you swap out the negative words for "I get to."

8. "I love to" - Notice the feeling that comes over you when you say that you love something. Maybe you start to smile. Your energy goes up and you feel terrific. The power of loving what you do trumps knowledge every time.

Now you have an overall understanding of how your brain, in its natural attempt to be efficient, can actually sabotage you. You also know that you have the ability to use *Radical Personal Responsibility* to shift your thoughts and your reality and take control of your success.

Next, let's next walk through a process of discovering the thoughts that are getting in the way of your success and the thoughts that will support you to live and lead with ease, grace and integrity.

Chapter 3

Your Magic Formula

People say that there is no such thing as magic. And yet, when my clients use the formula described in this chapter, they say that it feels like magic, because they go from feeling overwhelmed or stressed to being able to take control of their lives. Suddenly good things start to happen for them that they have no way of predicting. Life in general feels more easy and effortless. Sounds like magic to me.

What is the magic formula?

Now that you have an overall understanding of *Radical Personal Responsibility* and how it can benefit you, let's take a deeper dive into a formula that you can use to affect these types of changes in your life. First, I'll give you the 7-step formula to give you the complete picture. At the end of this chapter, I'll provide a shortcut you can use once you understand the full process.

To make it as clear as possible, I'll give you an example based on what happened when I was sent to work in the office back in the warehouse. At the same time, you can put the formula to use in a situation that isn't working for you.

Take a minute right now to get a piece of paper and pen and write down a sentence about a situation that isn't working for you. Keep it a simple concern, so that you will have a personal example and template for working through this process. The more you use this process, the more it will become second nature to you and the easier it will be for you to shift your thoughts in ways that serve you better.

Step 1: Start with where you are right now. Ask yourself, "What am I *thinking* about this situation?"

- In regards to my unexpected move to the warehouse office, my first thought was that I had spent the last 4 years working with my husband building up his business. We were focused on smaller local businesses. I was *rusty and out of touch* with what was happening for larger retailers.

- My second thought was that for the first time in my career, I was *at least 10 years older than everyone on my team*. I wasn't sure if I would be accepted by the team.

- Third, and in retrospect this is kind of funny, I had become accustomed to living and working in a southern atmosphere where the pace of the language was slower. The day I arrived on site, everyone seemed to be talking at warp speed. I couldn't understand them and I *wasn't sure that I was going to be able to fit into their culture*.

Step 2: Notice the emotions that are attached to your thoughts. Ask yourself, "What am I *feeling* when I have the thoughts I named in step #1?"

Ewwwww, emotions!!!

Who wants to talk about emotions? Most of us have learned that in business we have to squash or hide our emotions. Here is a little thought that might help you understand why this step is so important. Emotions are a combination of:

E (for Energy) + Motion = Emotion

If we are having negative emotions we don't have the energy to take action (or motion). If we have positive emotions our energy is much higher and we are more able to take the action that will support us to get where we want to go. Observing our E-Motions can help us to know if we will have the energy to take action or to be effective in our work. Emotions aren't something to wallow in or avoid. Emotions are simply indicators that our thoughts are either working for us or against us. Best of all, the moment we recognize our negative emotions and realize that we can shift them, we are on the verge of discovering something about our self and our thoughts that will make a huge difference in our work results!

Here is what I was feeling when I was asked to move to the office back in the warehouse.

- I was thinking that I was rusty and the emotion that was coming up for me was *anxious* - anxious that I wasn't going to cut the mustard.

- I was older than the rest of the team and I felt *disconnected* and *out of touch* with how they viewed the world.

- I was accustomed to a slower pace and I was *worried* that I might make a fool of myself or embarrass my team.

Step 3: Actions.

What did you DO when you had the thoughts you had in step #1 and the feelings you had in step #2? Or another way to ask the question is, "How do you do a specific emotion?" For instance, if you are feeling frustrated about a situation, do you avoid the situation, complain or use sarcasm, figure out a way to work around the problem, or talk to other people?

Example:
- *When I thought I was rusty and felt anxious, I hid.* Instead of getting really involved in what was happening around me, I stayed at my desk and worked really hard at a set of tasks. I tried to make everything perfect. I didn't share anything with others unless I was sure that I had worked out any possible mistakes.

- *When I felt disconnected and out of touch, I didn't reach out to others.* I stayed in my corner and didn't talk a lot. I didn't ask people to lunch or try to find out about them. I didn't share what I knew and I didn't spend time building camaraderie or team spirit.

- *When I felt out of place, I didn't speak up in meetings* with the client. I didn't make an attempt to connect with the client. I was quiet.

Wow – look how many times "I didn't" shows up. With all those negative thoughts, how could I have expected anything good to happen? Important to note is that I did none of this consciously. It was just the result of my thoughts and emotions regarding the situation I was in at the time.

Step 4: Ask yourself, "What about the thoughts, emotions and actions that I am having is disturbing, upsetting or eating away at my peace of mind?"

In mulling over the situation, there were several things that were eating away at me.

- First, I was clearly afraid that I might lose my job and my family needed my income. They were counting on me. What if I failed them? What if I failed myself? What then?

- Second, I was discouraged that after 20 years of working my way up the ladder and having led projects like this one, I found myself back at the beginning. What if this was it, that I was stuck creating flowcharts for the rest of my life?

- Third, I was having difficulty establishing good relations with the team and the client. What had changed in the four years I was away from these projects? Was I no longer capable of building relationships? Were people laughing at me?

Step 5: Discover your core thought or belief about yourself. Ask yourself, "If everything I have written down in the first four steps is true, then what does that say about me? What does it say about my character, or what does it say about my personal or public image?"

This is the toughest step, the step that means that we take responsibility. In fact, Radical Personal Responsibility for what is happening in our lives. Don't let it scare you off. This is also the pay dirt, the money, the gold at the end of the rainbow. Here's how it works.

I asked myself, "If it is true that I am in danger of losing my job, that I am stuck doing flowcharts for the rest of my life and that people may be laughing at me, what does that say about me?"

My first reaction was, "Well, I guess I am failing. Look at where I was going before and where I am now. How could I have let that happen?" (Not feeling so good right now.)

Then I asked myself again, "If it is true that I am failing, what does that say about me?"

My response this time was, "I guess that I just don't have what it takes to do the job anymore. Look how my project leader treated me. He must think I'm really useless. He was probably expecting a consultant with 20 years of experience to bring a lot to the table, and I don't seem to have what it takes anymore. And what was I doing instead? Sitting at my desk, silently working on tasks that a junior consultant could handle. Was he angry? Yes. Do I blame him? No. And did he trust me? What do you think? Is there any wonder that when he had the opportunity, he moved me to the office in the back?" (Feeling a little sorry for myself now.)

Then I asked myself again, "If it is true that I don't have what it takes to do the job anymore, what does that say about me?"

My answer was, "Wow, I must be getting old."

Again, the question, "If it is true that I am getting old, what does that say about me?"

My answer was: "Well, maybe I'm too old to be of value to a project like this anymore."

In order to get to my bottom line thought, it took several more rounds of asking myself if what I was thinking about myself was true.

Finally, a small voice in my head said, "You are not valuable anymore." Yuck! Hearing this voice in my head certainly didn't feel good at the time. In fact, it felt pretty rotten. Yes, this final answer had me feeling very sad and I cried inside myself.

However, little did I know at the time that what I had discovered was my core thought or belief about myself. Recognizing that I thought or believed that I wasn't valuable was the beginning of the most positive step in my life.

The great thing about discovering what it was that I believed about myself is that now I could change that key thought or belief. And so can you. You can change your thoughts, which will automatically change your emotions and change your actions. When you change your core thought or belief about yourself, your entire perspective on life will change and the reactions you are getting from the world will naturally change as well.

Step 6: Discover a new and empowering belief about yourself.

In order to change a belief about yourself, you first have to recognize that your belief is coming from a pattern that was developed in your subconscious brain in order to protect itself. Think back to some of the stories I've told you about my clients. In each case, they discovered a thought pattern that was developed as a mechanism of self-preservation of the brain. If this is confusing to you or if you skipped the chapter on how our brain works, I suggest that you stop now and go back and read about your brain. It will help you to work through this step.

If you are clear about how the brain is trying to protect itself, then you are ready to work through this discovery of your personal pattern that is no longer serving you.

First ask yourself the question, "What is the first time that I can recall having an experience that caused me to believe something negative about myself?"

Generally, our belief patterns start to develop when we are younger than six or seven years old. But it could happen at any time. For instance, one of the incidents I remember from my childhood that probably contributed to my thinking that I was no longer valuable was hearing my parents talking about one of my "old" relatives who couldn't keep a job.

Once you have an experience or learning situation in mind relative to your negative thought about yourself, write it down. You may not remember the very first time. It really doesn't matter. Just write down the incident you do remember. What is important is: You start to see that it is a thought pattern and to separate that pattern from who you really are as a person.

Next, write down as many similar experiences or learnings as you can think of in your life. Some of my clients find that it is helpful to create a visual time line of their experiences. You can do this easily by getting a piece of brown wrapping paper or a big poster board. Draw a time line the length of the paper. Every five to ten years put a mark on the paper and label it. On the bottom half of the timeline write down similar experiences or learnings that happened in each five- to ten-year spot. The more you can think of, the easier it will be to see the pattern that your brain has created to protect itself and you.

Now, move to the topside of time line and write down learnings and experiences that show that your belief about yourself isn't true. This will help you to see that your belief isn't you, it is just a core thought or belief that your brain has stored in your subconscious, and you get to choose what you want to believe.

Step 7: Choose a new thought that supports you now. Ask yourself, "What belief can I have that will better support what I want to happen in my life?"

Example:
The belief I shifted was from "I'm out of touch and not valuable anymore" to "I am valuable, and with my experience and knowledge, I have a lot to offer."

That shift in belief supported a shift in other thoughts and then in my emotions and actions. The thoughts that shifted were that I was rusty, out of touch, and couldn't adapt to the client environment.

Then I looked for signs that I was valuable. What I came to recognize was that the reason I was hired for the project was that the people who hired me thought of me as able to bring value to the project. For example, I realized:

- The people who hired me weren't concerned about my age. In fact, my age could have been an advantage. The client saw me as experienced and knowledgeable, and they were looking for my input.

- No one cared if I talked with a southern accent as long as I brought value to the project. In fact, after a short while I mentioned to a client that I was struggling a bit with the speed of their conversations and it became a friendly joke. One client would see me coming down the hall and would say to his colleague in a very sloooow drawl, "Here comes that souuuuthern gaaaal. We had better slooow dooown our talking." And then we would all laugh.

As soon as I shifted my core belief to "I am valuable," new thoughts emerged and then my emotions changed from anxious, disconnected and worried to feeling energized, engaged in my work and excited about the possibilities. Night and day, wouldn't you say?

Help for sticky stituations.

To be perfectly honest, sometimes we find ourselves in situations where we are stuck on a specific belief and we have trouble shaking it. If that happens to you, here are a few questions to help open up your mind to other ways of thinking about your situation.

1. How are you different from when you were in a similar situation the first time? If you have been in a similar situation and it didn't work out for you, do you believe that this situation will turn out the same way, that there is nothing you can do about it? What is different about you now, and how would those differences affect your outcome?

For example, when I was a Girl Scout we had to go door-to-door selling cookies. I made a mistake in asking for the wrong amount of money and had to go back to each person and ask for more money. With that experience as a young girl, it isn't difficult to see why I believed that selling was difficult and why I avoided it. But that was then, and it was my first experience selling. If asked to sell Girl Scout cookies now I would probably find it enjoyable, because I love meeting people and almost everyone loves Girl Scout cookies. Simply stated, I'm not the person that I was when I had my first experience.

2. How are you limiting yourself by your beliefs? When you get into a situation where you think that you don't have what it takes to do something, take a few minutes to write down what makes you capable of being successful, instead of only looking at what you think you can't do. Another way to let go of limiting thoughts is to ask yourself, "What would be the thought that would move me forward in this situation?" or "What is a belief that I could have that would remove these limitations?"

A number of years ago I was working on a project with a national pharmacy retailer. I was scheduled to be in a meeting with the executive sponsor. All night I had been sweating this meeting, believing that I didn't have the experience to be as effective as I wanted to be. On the drive to the meeting, I had a shift in my thought. I had recently heard something about taking a situation you feared and finding a way to be grateful for it. As I thought about the situation, I recognized that I wanted to move from project manager to program manager. That would mean becoming more comfortable interacting with the corporate executives. Instead of being fearful about the situation, I became grateful for the opportunity.

What was intended to be a thirty-minute review ended up in a two-hour session, and I came away with several potential opportunities to help my client and bring in business for my company. If that sounds a bit like a Pollyanna story, keep in mind how quickly she was able to turn a bad situation into a good situation. Some days it still amazes me how effective it is to shift my thoughts to gratitude and how quickly the situation improves.

3. How is this negative belief serving me? We know that the negative belief was planted in our subconscious to protect us at some point in our life. But what if we discover the thought pattern and core belief but don't want to take *Radical Personal Responsibility* for our thoughts, emotions and actions? Chances are that the negative belief is serving us in some way.

For instance, I have for most of my life avoided putting my expense reports together until the last minute. I have been great at coming up with all kinds of excuses like "I'm too busy." Logically I know that this is crazy talk and that it is putting more pressure on me when I wait until the last minute to do this work. On the other hand, in an odd way, it gets me off the hook. I don't have to blame myself or think less of myself if "I'm busy." What if I stopped blaming myself and just took responsibility?

I'll be honest here. I still haven't worked this one out completely. And that is OK. This process doesn't mean that a magic wand is waved and SHAZAMM, everything is different now. What it does mean is that we are aware and that if we want to make our life easier, we have the process to do so if we choose to take *Radical Personal Responsibility*.

Make a decision, be committed and take the first small step.

You now have the 7 steps that you can use to shift your reality every time you find yourself in a situation that isn't working for you. As I mentioned at the beginning of this chapter, the first few times you use this process, it will take some time. But do it a few times and you will find that you will move through it faster and faster. In fact, most people find that after a while, they know their core belief and can shift it on a dime, because the same underlying thought comes up over and over. In addition, the more you use the process, the more you will find that your work and in fact all of your life is working out just the way you want it to turn out.

If you think that the process is not working as effectively as you hoped it would, there are three little steps you can take that will help cement the change you want to make in your perspective.

Make a firm decision.

The first step is to make a firm decision or commitment to you and to your new belief about yourself. A coaching group I facilitate was talking about creating a vision for our futures. One person suggested that we create vision boards to help us focus on what we want to create in our lives. That is a great idea on the surface. The downside is that often we have a vision of what we want but we don't fully commit to making the changes. Or we overcommit and spend a lot of energy taking massive action, and we wear ourselves out in the process or give up entirely.

What I am suggesting is that you make a firm decision. It was my firm decision to not spend the rest of my career in a back office creating flow charts that catapulted me forward. What firm decision do you need to make right now that will move you forward? When you have an answer, ask yourself, "When do I want to make that change? If not now, when?"

Take one small step forward.

Once we make a firm decision to change, it is important to reinforce our decision by taking immediate action. One of the first steps I took was to turn that warehouse office into what in consulting is often referred to as a war room. It was a long room with a large table, surrounded by white boards. I suggested to my boss that this was the perfect place to hold strategy sessions. Soon it became the project meeting hub, and the image of that warehouse office improved dramatically, as did my role on the team.

I committed to taking steps to change the circumstances. Small steps can lead to big changes. What actions can you take right now that will reflect your new thoughts and emotions?

Don't wait. Take that first step now. The longer you wait to take the steps you need to make in order to change your situation, the more difficult it feels.

Celebrate Your Success

Celebrate! You deserve it! Pat yourself on the back. Don't wait until the results are in. Celebrate that you recognized a thought that was getting in the way of your success and are ready to shift it now. Call a friend and tell her about your success. Take a night off and relax. Whatever you do, celebrate your shift in thought. So much of our lives we focus on what isn't going right. It's a trained response that most of us picked up as children. Recognizing and celebrating what we do right for ourselves is a way to encourage ourselves to keep moving forward. Go ahead - Celebrate! You deserve it!

Next Steps

This sounds great, doesn't it? And it doesn't seem hard to do! Yes, it did help me to have coaches to help me move through this process faster and who could help me discover the thoughts and emotions that I was struggling to uncover. But I have to tell you, when I discovered and started putting *Radical Personal Responsibility* to work, I felt like a SuperWoman, as though nothing could stop me. I am forever grateful to Paul and Layne Cutright, who introduced me to the concept of *Radical Personal Responsibility*.

Unfortunately, or perhaps I can say fortunately, this isn't the end of the story. On the exterior, I looked really successful. The status was there and the pay was on target. And work did come together more easily for me.

However, inside I was still a mess. While I was working on the third project that I mentioned earlier, the one where I was in charge of an entire project, I found myself working 60- to 70-hour weeks in an attempt to implement a 12-month project in 6 months' time. Sound familiar? We were very successful, but my mind and my body were totally overwhelmed. No matter what I did, I carried a nagging feeling that something was wrong. When I finally took a day off from work to see a doctor, I was diagnosed with a pre-cancerous condition. If you've ever been diagnosed with a serious disease, you know how quickly it can change your perspective on life.

Luckily for me, because of my own experience of working with a coach, I had already decided that I was going to start working towards becoming a coach myself. At that point, I took a year-long journey with iPEC (Institute for Professional Excellence in Coaching), where I discovered a concept first developed by psychologist Bruce Schneider called Energy Leadership. What I learned was a reflection of what Einstein said over 100 years ago, "Everything is energy." Every thought we have is associated with a different level of mental, emotional and physical energy, and our energy can either be negative/catabolic or positive/anabolic. It can either tear us down mentally, emotionally and physically, or build us up. Not only does energy affect ourselves, it also touches everyone we come into contact with and affects their mental, emotional and physical health as well.

In essence, what I learned that year is that it isn't enough to just be aware of our beliefs, thoughts, emotions and actions. We have to know what beliefs and thoughts are hurting us and what thoughts are helping us and know how to shift them to work for us instead of against us.

In learning how to shift my thoughts from negative energy to positive energy, I was able to turn my physical health around and I discovered how I could work as a woman and at the same time be successful in the technology field. I discovered that I didn't have to be Superwoman. I could be my authentic self. I could laugh, think and act like a woman and still be successful. I call what I discovered: WiseWoman Leadership.

Magic Formula – A Shortcut

Often people will tell me they are stressed, frustrated or overwhelmed. If we can name or identify our feelings, they can be a shortcut to discovering what thoughts we need to change to improve our situation. After you've worked through the 7 step process, try the shortcut below.

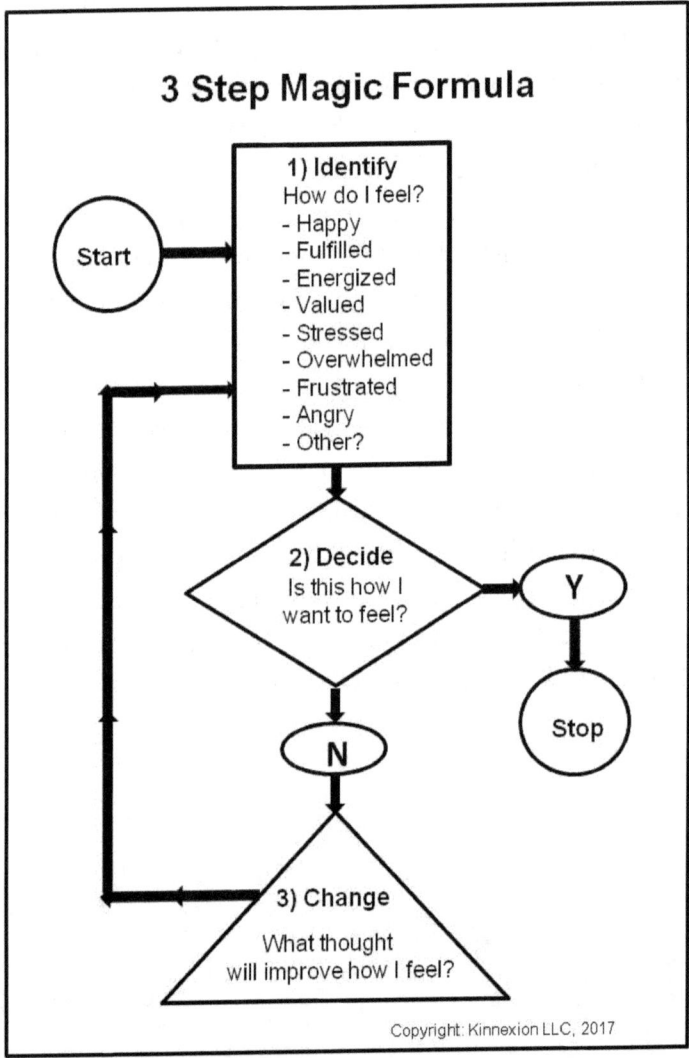

Step 2
Choose Your Perspective

Chapter 4

The First Step to WiseWoman Leadership

In the first three chapters, we looked at the big picture of how our brain works and what can happen when we shift our thoughts. And we discovered a magic formula for making those shifts.

In this chapter, we start to look at specific categories or levels of thought and how they affect our emotions, our actions and the results that we get as leaders. We will also look at the advantages and disadvantages of each level of thought and how you can move through each level to the next. In addition, in these next few chapters you will start to get an understanding of where you are on the journey to being a WiseWoman Leader.

Defining WiseWoman Leadership

Hopefully, if you are reading this book, you think of yourself as a leader or at least a potential leader. Many people, when they picture a leader, are inclined to think of CEOs of large companies, heads of state or military leaders. However, for purposes of this book, we define the label "leader" more broadly.

A leader is a person who has the ability to influence people to make a commitment and take action, including influencing our self.

For simplicity's sake, let's say that this morning you got yourself out of bed and opened this book in order to learn something new. In other words, you lead yourself to make a commitment and take an action. By definition, that means that everyone reading this book is a leader or you wouldn't be here. Can we agree on that definition for now? Since by definition anyone reading this book is a leader, the more important question becomes: How effective are we as a leader? This is where energy comes in to play.

WiseWoman Leadership is based on Einstein's theory that everything is energy. The food you eat is energy, the chair you are sitting in is energy, and you are energy. Even your thoughts are energy.

Maybe you are a physicist and agree totally with Einstein, and then again, maybe not. However, before you think that I have gone off the deep end into the la-la land of woo-woo theories and shut this book, let me explain what I mean so that it makes practical sense. To help explain the relationship of energy to leadership, let's take a minute to experience what we mean by energy.

Stop here for a minute and think of a really bad day in your life. Picture it in your mind. Maybe it was a day that you lost a client or a job. Or maybe you lost something more personal, like a family member or good friend. Get a really clear picture of that day in your mind.

Notice how you feel when you think about this situation. That memory takes the wind out of your sails, doesn't it? What is your face doing? Are you smiling or are the edges of your lips turned downward? How is your body responding? Is it a bit slumped or just quiet? What about your energy level? Is it high or low? I'm guessing your energy is lower than average. If it was a really sad day, you may even get a tear in your eye.

Now switch the picture. Think about a really great day in your life. Picture the day you finally signed that important new client, you got a new job, you started a wonderful relationship, maybe you got married, had a baby. Do you have a clear picture of that day? Woo-hoo! Life was great! How do you feel now? Do you feel lighter and more like smiling? Have you shifted the way you are sitting or standing? Do you notice more of what is going on around you? How is your energy now?

There are three things you'll want to notice about this exercise.

- First, let's say you need to influence someone to take some action and get things done. Do you think you would be more effective if you had low energy or high energy? High energy, of course. That means that in order to be more effective leaders, we need to be able to raise our energy on demand.

- Second, notice that it was the shift in your thoughts that caused the shift in your energy. It was your thought about a bad day or a good day that shifted your emotions, your actions and your energy.

- Third, I invited you to change your thoughts and you had the power to do so. You didn't hesitate. You simply changed your thoughts. That means that you have within you the power at any time to choose your thoughts, raise your energy and more effectively lead and influence people to take action, including yourself.

Taking the definition of leader and adding the effect that energy has on leadership, we come up with a definition of WiseWoman Leadership.

WiseWoman Leadership is using our ability to choose our thoughts at will and to choose thoughts that raise our energy, so that we are able to more easily and effectively influence people to make a commitment and to take action, including our own self.

Choosing Our Thoughts

Now that we have a definition of WiseWoman Leadership, the next question becomes which thoughts (or core beliefs) do we choose in order to raise our energy and be more influential?

WiseWoman Leadership is broken down into 7 levels of thought. Each level is at a progressively higher level of energy. Each level is associated with a core thought, emotion and action. Each level has both advantages and disadvantages.

In the next few chapters we will look at each level in detail, with examples and stories of real people and the thoughts they needed to shift in order to raise their energy and be more influential.

In this chapter, we will start with Level 1 thinking. It is the level most frequently associated with stress. Stress is the number one complaint that I get from my clients about their work environment. Possibly that is true for you as well.

Stress is also the number one trigger for dis-ease, especially chronic metabolic diseases like cardiac arrest, diabetes and fibromyalgia. That makes it even more important to understand the thoughts that are underlying this level of thinking. Once we recognize the thoughts that are creating a negative environment, it is easier to shift our thoughts to ones that are more beneficial.

Level 1 – The Victim

Some of the biggest complaints that I hear from women working in technology is that they are not respected. I was working at a technology event one Saturday. The woman who was in charge of the event told me that her boss, a man, expects her to get the coffee and take the notes, even though she is the team leader. One of my clients complained that all the extra work, especially the drudge work, always ends up on her desk. At a WITI (Women in Technology International) board meeting one evening, the conversation turned to work and several women said that when they are in a meeting and offer an idea, they are often ignored and sometimes their ideas are stolen.

There is some truth in what these women say. I certainly wouldn't argue with the women who say that working in a male-dominated industry is a challenge.

However, it is critical that you understand what I am about to say if you want to fully enjoy your work and be successful working in technology or any other male-dominated industry.

If you consider the complaints of the women above, it becomes evident that these women feel like what is happening is out of their control, that there is nothing they can do about their situation. I believe that one of the biggest reasons so many women end up leaving the industry is not because they can't do something, but because they believe they can't change the situation. And yes, there are situations where decisions are made based on subconscious perceptions rather than fact. That being said, there are many (and in my experience, most) circumstances where we have way more ability than we think we have to influence a situation.

Not finding a different way to think or approach a negative situation and instead simply accepting it, complaining or avoiding the situation, is exactly what Level 1 thinking is about.

Level 1 is often referred to as the level of the Victim.

I'm not really crazy about the label **Victim**. To me, it insinuates that we were attacked or that we are lying around in bed all day, whining and popping chocolates in our mouth, and I don't see that happening with most people.

What is meant by **Victim** is that we think that things are happening to us that are out of our control, that there is nothing we can do to change the situation.

- **The underlying thought of the Victim is "I lose."**
- The key emotions are stress and overwhelm.
- The primary action we take is to avoid. We may actually be very busy but avoid doing what needs to be done to have our needs met.
- The primary advantage is feeling safe in situations where we feel uncomfortable or have fear about the future or regrets about past actions.
- The disadvantage is that, even though we may expend a lot of physical and mental effort, it is difficult to get our needs fully met.

This level can be a little tricky to identify, because we may look very busy and lose ourselves in our work, and at the same time we may avoid doing the one thing we need to do in order to get our needs met. Think about the person who is busy with paperwork but never makes the critical call to the important client. Or there was the time as a team leader that I needed an extra person on my team, but instead of asking for one, I worked longer hours so I wouldn't rock the boat.

Here is another way to think about Level 1. Let's say that there is a room with a big window and you can see through that window that there is a delicious meal about to be served. You are hungry and want to have some of that food. However, between you and the room with the food is a door that is shut and appears to be locked. If I am at Level 1, I might:

- Expend an enormous amount of energy thinking about how to open the door but never get to the point of actually trying to open the door.

- Perhaps I try to open the door but I don't put my full weight behind it and give up when it doesn't easily open.
- I might study the door looking for possible ways to open the door and blame myself for not being able to figure out how to open it. Or I might blame someone else who I think should have showed me how to open the door.
- Or I might think that if the door is shut, then I'm not supposed to take part in the meal and give up before I even start.
- Or I may get caught in the trap of thinking that I don't know enough about opening doors and need to keep studying how to open a door before I give it a try.

How might Level 1 look in real life? Let's look at one of the biggest complaints that I hear from women, which is that people ignore and/or steal our ideas. How can Level 1 thinking affect our ability to be heard? Below are several Level 1 approaches that many women subconsciously use when they are in a situation where they want to share an idea. See if you recognize yourself or any other women in one of the responses to a situation. The situation is that a team is talking through how to handle a technical problem.

1. A woman on the team wants to share her idea for a solution. She is uncertain as to whether it will be accepted. Finally, she blurts out her idea during a quiet spot in the conversation. However, everyone else is still processing something that had been said just prior and they ignore her. To her it feels like they have slighted her, but what is actually happening is that she is allowing her uncertainty to keep her from being present to the conversation. Subconsciously, someone in the group hears her idea and without realizing where the idea came from brings it up later at an appropriate moment. Now she feels like her idea has been stolen.

2. Another woman says to the group that she has a great idea. People turn to her. However, she is not certain they will agree with her, and she overcompensates by telling a long story or giving lots of information. She takes forever to get to the point. To the team, this feels like inaction and is frustrating, and mentally they turn her off.

3. Another woman wants to share a thought but hesitates for a fraction of a second. Energetically, people sense that she is not confident about her idea, and before she can even begin, the team has subconsciously decided that her idea isn't going to fly. The hesitation is so subtle that it may be hard to believe that it could make that big a difference, but think about the difference between these two sentences and you will understand what is happening. One little comma, and the entire situation is turned on its head.

> Let's eat, Grandma.
> Let's eat Grandma.

The commonality in all three of these situations is the subconscious thought or belief that their idea might be rejected, and by association they would be rejected. This is a huge roadblock for women. We tend to associate having our ideas rejected with being personally rejected. The key thought that has to shift in these situations is that we are valuable, even when one of our ideas is rejected.

Another scenario where I have seen Level 1 thinking get in the way of women progressing in their careers is how they interact with people who are in authority, especially men. For instance, let's say the CEO of a major corporation is coming in to meet the people at a local office. Everyone is excited to meet him and wants to make an impression on him.

1. One woman starts right in telling him everything she knows, including all her ideas and how great her team is doing. She is nervous about being accepted, and her subconscious (or conscious) hope is that he will see how valuable she is to the company. However, she has skipped having a friendly preliminary conversation, and the general result is that she appears unfriendly and might be seen as a braggart.

2. Another woman walks up and vigorously shakes his hand, hoping that he will see that she is "man enough" for the job. Her approach feels unnatural to the receiver, and he may wonder if she is always this "pushy."

3. Another woman waits patiently in line hoping that she will get to talk with him and that he will see how considerate she is and what a great team player she is being. Chances are she never gets to talk with the CEO.

4. A fourth woman uses flirting to get his attention (yes, flirting...I've seen this happen many times), hoping that he will see how friendly and easy to get along with she is. He may enjoy the flirting but ignore her when she presents a serious idea.

In each example above, the woman has avoided being her authentic self. I generally see people avoiding being authentic when they are nervous or lack enough confidence. Avoiding in any form is Level 1 thinking. Avoiding being our authentic self has the same effect as if we are wearing a mask. People subconsciously sense that they can't see what is going on behind the mask, so they don't trust us or have as much confidence in us.

Many of you may be thinking, I know women like this, but

they are definitely not me. I would never avoid doing what needs to get done or flirt to get attention, etc. I'm a seasoned leader and I wouldn't be where I am if I avoided what needed to be done to succeed. True enough. However, as I mentioned earlier, Level 1 thinking can be tricky, because it can look like you are doing everything "right," but internally it could be that you are not fully committed and lack of commitment comes from Level 1 thinking. Let's look a couple of real life examples to understand what I mean.

Samantha's Fortune 500 proposal

One of my coaching clients and her partner were getting ready to deliver a proposal to a Fortune 500 company. It was a terrific opportunity to move their company to a new level of business. She had come to me for some coaching because she was concerned about the inconsistent response she was getting from the client and was hoping that we might discover the missing link.

We spent some time talking through some of the typical preparation questions, such as: Do you completely understand the client's needs? Does the client have any hidden agendas? What allows you to stand out from other vendors? What is unique about your proposition that will make a big difference for the client? What does the client think is missing from your proposal that might cause the client to choose another vendor? Does the client seem genuinely interested in hearing your proposal? Does your presentation align with the client's expectations? Is your presentation well thought out and engaging?

As you can probably imagine, our conversation went on for some time and ended with my client saying, "Well, we'll just have to see."

At which point I said, "Whoa, hold on a second. I'm curious, what do you mean by 'Well, we'll just have to see'?"

In this one simple, very non-descript statement, we discovered the missing link. She didn't say, "This is going to knock their socks off." Or "This is our best proposal yet." Or even something like, "OK, we're ready to meet this challenge." She said, "Well, we'll just have to see."

Here is the question I asked her next. "If you were deciding between two vendors and they were equally experienced, equally talented, equally skilled, had equal pricing, both had amazing ideas and great approaches…how would you know whom to choose?"

Commitment

Personally, I would look for the company that to me seemed more committed. OK, you might be thinking, I can buy into that concept. But how do we recognize who is more committed? To clarify, let's begin by defining what we mean by the word commitment.

The word commitment comes from the Latin word 'committere' which means, to join, to bring together or to connect. When we deliver a proposal (or any other message), the word commitment means that our words and our actions are in sync or connected. If our words and actions are out of sync, then we are not fully committed and lack of commitment is always based on Level 1 thinking.

For instance, have you ever watched a newscaster talking about a disaster and the whole time they were smiling? It's weird, isn't it? Maybe the smile is genuine, but it is out of sync with their words. That shows a lack of commitment. Perhaps the newscaster is concerned that they aren't good enough, so they cover their insecurity by putting on a "cheerful" face.

What do we do, as the audience, when this happens? On the surface, we may do nothing. But internally, our authenticity barometer goes up, and we may silently disregard either the newscaster or what they are saying.

What about the person who has had an amazing technological breakthrough that could make a huge difference for the world, and they read about it from a script or from PowerPoint slides in a deadpan tone without much expression or enthusiasm? Do you find yourself yawning, tuning out and wishing the presentation was over? Again, this shows a lack of commitment on the part of the presenter, which is Level 1 thinking. What is interesting is that when a presenter is not committed to their material, the reaction from the audience tends to be noncommittal as well, to both the presenter and their ideas.

By comparison, if we are fully committed to our client and to our products or services, then we will be enthusiastic, we will be inspired by the opportunity to make a difference for our client, and we will express our enthusiasm in our words and our actions. The benefits that the client will receive will be so clear and compelling in our mind that we cannot help but raise our client's energy as well.

OK, I can almost hear you saying it: "But, Jane, this is a large corporation we are dealing with and we need to be professional. We can't get carried away with our enthusiasm." Yes, you are right. We always want to be appropriate for the situation. However, if being professional means damping down our emotions to the point where our client cannot hear, see and experience our commitment to serving them, then we have missed the point and very possibly a big opportunity and…this is Level 1 thinking.

A critical part of your success

Commitment, or shifting out of Level 1 thinking, is such a critical part of our success in any arena that I feel a need to share one more example.

Let's say you are responsible for staffing a huge project. Getting the right people on board will either make or break the project.

You interview two different people for a job. They have equal qualifications. Who do you choose? Do you choose the person who is pitch-perfect yet stone-faced serious and highly controlled in their response? Or do you choose the person who is pitch-perfect and also practically bubbling with enthusiasm about making a difference for your project? Who do you think is more committed?

Did I just hear you say, "Well, duh – the person who is enthusiastic." What makes this so? Because the words they speak and the enthusiasm with which they deliver their words (i.e., their actions) are in sync. We know instinctively that they think differently, and it is that thinking and the associated energy that we buy into, not the details.

Doesn't it seem obvious when put this way? And yet, when we get into a situation where our future is on the line and we know we are being judged by our client, what often happens? We get caught up in trying to make things *perfect* and forget that one of the key things our clients look for from us is our commitment to them.

Oh yeah, perfectionism. Raise your hand if you have ever felt plagued by that devil of a thought. Mine hand is up there with you, so don't feel like you are alone. How do we get past perfectionism and to a sense of commitment? By recognizing the thoughts behind the perfectionism – thoughts like "I'm not smart enough or valuable enough or experienced enough" – and learning to shift our thoughts to recognizing how truly valuable we are to others.

Kate doesn't get paid

One of the biggest concerns with Level 1 thinking is not always the immediate results but what it does to our psyche over the long term. We can go from not being fully committed to expecting perfection of ourselves, and on to blaming ourselves for everything that goes wrong. It can drag us down to the point where we can't see a solution, even when it is right in front of us.

A client of mine, I'll call her Kate, had a new business. Kate had made a connection with a person who was giving her referrals. It was a terrific opportunity for her to grow her business and she was doing a great job following through with the referrals. The only problem was that the referral source was also the go-between for the financial end of the arrangement and wasn't paying Kate on a timely basis. This caused a lot of stress for Kate, who was struggling to keep her head above water, as do many new businesses.

Kate put up with the situation for at least 6 months. Even though it was very stressful, she didn't want to rock the boat and risk losing her referral source, so she avoided confronting them. When money would get tight, she would put off making critical expenditures like getting her car serviced. You can probably imagine what happened next.

One morning she went to leave for a meeting and her car wouldn't start. That put her in danger of losing clients. Even with this critical incident, she still didn't say anything to the referral source. Why not?

When people are victims, sometimes they blame themselves for anything negative that is going on in their lives. In other words, they spend more time looking at what they might be doing wrong than in taking action to change the situation. Kate wondered if perhaps she wasn't doing a good job with her clients and if they were complaining to her resource, and that was the reason she wasn't getting paid on time. She was afraid to bring up her concerns with her resource and to find out if that was true. Meanwhile, her clients were all telling her how much they appreciated her. Who was she to believe, her clients or the voice in her head that was telling her she wasn't good enough?

At the time, her business was new and she had not built her self-confidence to a place where she believed her clients. She also hadn't planned for it to take as long as it had to build her business, and financially she was constantly in survival mode. She found herself in a situation where she literally couldn't breathe. The situation was not only causing financial problems, it was causing her to lose sleep and it was affecting her health.

When Kate and I talked, we discovered that the only time she was getting paid was when she went to the office of her referral source and waited around for them to take the time to write her a check. In other words, chances were good that not getting paid regularly had little or nothing to do with Kate's abilities or performance and more do with the business organization of her source.

Once Kate stopped blaming herself for what was happening, she could see that she had options and could decide on an action that would best support her needs. Should she spend three hours a week driving to that office and waiting around for a check? Should she put up with the situation and just hope it got better? Should she remove herself from the situation all together?

In the end, Kate decided that until her business was full and she had enough clients that she was attracting without the referral resource, she would spend the three hours a week going to that office. That had a surprise ending. Not only did she relieve a lot of personal financial tension because she was getting paid regularly, but because she spent time in the office, her referral source had her more at top of mind and gave her additional referrals.

Up-Leveling

With each of these examples, there is one common denominator. The person did not have to wait until something outside of her changed. She made a conscious decision to change the thoughts going on in her head or her perspective on the situation, and everything related to the situation changed as well.

The good news is that you have the same capacity to shift your thinking and raise your energy and change what is happening in your world. That means taking time to become aware of your thoughts or, as mentioned in an earlier chapter, to take *Radical Personal Responsibility*.

To help you get started, I've made a list of some of the most common things that my clients have said to me that are Level 1 energy. See if you recognize any of these in yourself. If you do recognize a statement that you commonly use, don't think about it as something you did wrong. Remember that it is a thought pattern that you have developed over many years and that your brain wants to hold onto because it thinks it is protecting you, even when that thought no longer serves you. Look at your awareness of the negative thought as your opportunity to shift your thoughts to a higher level of thinking and feeling and being in the world. Think about everything that will change once you make the decision to change your thoughts.

Here is the short list. My suggestion is that you read it out loud. If you agree with the statement or a statement doesn't feel good, it probably means that it is worth paying attention to for you. Take this thought and go back to chapter three on the Magic Formula and follow it through to up your thinking level.

Level 1 Thoughts

- My boss keeps dumping more and more work on me.
- I can't say no to work from my boss. I may lose my job, not be promoted, make my boss angry.
- I should have known better than to get involved in this project,

take this job, spend that money.
- I feel like everyone is after me for something. I'm so overwhelmed with work and home life. It's impossible to balance things out.
- I changed jobs thinking it was going to be better and it is starting all over again, with my boss loading extra work on me.
- Whenever I give a presentation or make a suggestion, the guys in the room act like I am an idiot.
- I give my boss an idea and he just ignores me.
- I try to get information about some new piece of technology and the guys laugh at me or ignore me.
- How am I supposed to get ahead if all the decisions are being made in the men's room?
- I don't think that my boss/company/client cares about anything other than the bottom line. My job feels so purposeless.
- I should never have done that or gone down that road.
- If only I had taken that other job, not made that mistake, followed through more thoroughly.
- I looked at the job description and realized that I don't have all the experience they are looking for in this position. They want so much and I'm just not capable of doing everything they want done.
- I have made some really dumb mistakes. Some days I hate myself for being so stupid.
- I'm so exhausted from everything that I have on my plate.
- Dang, another mess. I cannot seem to do anything right today.
- The world is such a mess. There is so much suffering and pain everywhere I look.
- Women are always the underdog at work. Men always expect that we are going to get the coffee and take the notes.
- That's good enough. (As in, "Why bother trying?")
- Guess I'll just have to wait and see what happens.

- I sent the proposal. Whatever happens, it's out of my control now.
- Going into that room and making that mistake in front of everyone was so humiliating /embarrassing.
- I feel like SuperWoman with a bunch of kryptonite in my briefcase. All day long, all I do is push boulders up mountains by myself, go to bed, and then get up and do it all over again the next day.

Chapter 5

Fighting Your Way to the Top

A number of years ago, I was in Dallas on a project. A co-worker and I were talking over dinner. She told me how hard it was to keeping working when she felt like she was always fighting to be heard. She told me how hard it was to balance her work and her home life. Then she told me how hard it was to watch her father become more and more disabled.

After the third time she used the word "hard" about a situation, I started counting. In a 10-minute conversation, she used the word hard 15 times. I stopped her for a minute and asked her if she was aware that she used the word "hard" so many times. Her response was that to her *life is hard* and that she feels like she is constantly *fighting* to stay in balance at work and home. This is Level 2 thinking.

Level 2 thinking is called the Fighter.

- **The primary thought of the Fighter is "You lose."**
- The emotions are conflict, frustration, anger, resentment.
- The action is to push any barriers out of the way in order to get our needs met.
- The advantage of the **Fighter** is that it is a higher level of energy than the **Victim,** and unlike the victim, it allows us to move forward and get our needs met.
- The disadvantage is that when we are being the **Fighter**, it can be difficult to form strong business relationships and the results we get, although they may meet our basic needs, never really feel satisfying.

The **Fighter** can look like yelling, sarcasm or complaining. When we hear labels like "The bitch" (ladies) or "What a Jerk" (gentlemen), that is usually the Level 2 **Fighter** being displayed.

However, the most insidious form of the **Fighter** is not external. It is internal conflict. It goes quietly about wreaking havoc in our lives. It looks like life being hard or a struggle.

Do you remember the story about Kate from the last chapter? She was the person who wasn't getting paid on time by her referral source. When her car broke down and she didn't have the money to pay to fix it, she became frustrated. She wanted to sit down with her source and demand they pay her promptly, because she deserved to be treated with respect and she needed to be paid. On the other hand, she was concerned that she might lose her referral source, so she would back away from confronting them. Can you see how we can be in conflict with ourselves?

Let's go back to the analogy of that delicious meal that you can see through the window of the room with the locked door. When you are a **Fighter**, the tendency is to try to break through the locked door to get to the other side. We might push against the door with all our might. If it doesn't move, we get angry and frustrated. Or maybe we bang on the door over and over until our fists are bruised. We don't recognize that we have a choice in how to approach the door. Instead, we blame someone else or talk sarcastically about the idiot who locked the door in the first place.

Whatever hurt we experience, we don't give up fighting until we get our needs met. When we are at Level 2 thinking, it may look like anger, frustration or resentment, but the motivation underneath these feelings is a deep fear that our needs won't be met. When we act out of fear, we may get our initial needs met, but it generally isn't satisfying. It feels like surviving but not thriving.

As for leading others, being a fighter can make it very difficult to inspire people or gain their commitment. Forcing action using

Fighter thoughts, emotions and actions may work temporarily to move a situation forward in an emergency. At the same time, the **Fighter** creates feelings of dissatisfaction and distrust, which leads to an unproductive work environment and high turnover rates.

Again, it isn't always obvious when we are thinking at Level 2, especially if we have been trained to hold in our emotions. Let's look at a couple examples of leaders who are at Level 2 thinking.

The struggle for control

For 6 months, I had participated on a team planning for what we believed would be very positive change for an organization. Even though this meant taking on additional work outside of our regular schedules, we were excited about the potential and very willing to put in whatever time it took to reach our goal. The CEO of the organization had been very supportive and consistently encouraged us to move forward with our plans. That is, until the week that the CEO changed his tune.

This particular week, the CEO walked into our meeting and suddenly out of nowhere announced that another project is now taking precedence over our project in terms of funding, and we have to cut our budget by 1/3.

Some of the pieces of the old system were broken and had already been pulled out for replacement, and we have no choice but to go ahead with our project. The team believes we can take one of two actions. We can continue moving forward with the project as is and hope that we can get funding through another source, or we need to cut back our project to the point that when completed we will not have made any real progress and instead will be trudging along with another version of the same old system.

The elephant in the room

Now we get to what I perceive to be the elephant in the room. What has gone unspoken is that the CEO has become involved in the details of the project and is acting as the messenger between two different teams who are working at opposing goals (i.e., another form of the **Fighter** syndrome). You may be thinking, so what, isn't that the CEO's job, to mediate between the groups?

In the short view, being involved in detailed budgeting discussions and playing messenger between teams may appear to be the role that the CEO needs to take in order to keep control of the finances and keep projects moving forward. However, in the longer view, what happens when the leader lets go of the role of the visionary leader and instead gets mired in the details?

First, if a leader gets mired in the details and doesn't hold out a strong vision, then without even realizing it and most likely not meaning to, the leader starts to take sides. Without a mutually agreed upon vision as a guide in the decision-making process, people will always take sides. It is a normal and natural response to see everything from our personal perspective. That very normal response by the leader sets up a competition of sorts and subconsciously encourages the team members or different teams to also take sides. When the teams take sides, they can easily get stuck in thinking that there are only two ways to move forward: your way or my way. They can become blind to all the other possible solutions. The fight is on.

Second, without a strong vision being held up in front of people on a consistent basis, it is very easy for teams to get stuck working the same details over and over, arguing about personal opinions and never coming to a decision. When that happens, teams frequently bump up against time limits or get into a financial crunch. At that point, there may be no other choice but to make a quick and expedient decision, which generally only satisfies some of the people on the team. The team members who don't get their needs met end up not as engaged, and the organization as a whole suffers by being less effective. Ultimately, the decision that the team makes fails to truly meet anyone's needs.

Finally, what I perceive to be the biggest concern for leaders has to do with how the leader makes their teams feel. I know, I can almost hear you saying it, we are at work and we aren't supposed to feel, or at least not show our feelings. But in real life, we all know that it doesn't play out that way. For instance, when the CEO walked into our meeting after 6 months of supporting our plan and bluntly told our team that we had to cut our budget by 1/3, we immediately felt deflated and devalued. The looks on people's faces were at first flat and unexpressive as they quite obviously tried to contain their emotions. Then there was anger, frustration and fighting back. Worst of all was the loss of trust in the CEO. How did the lack of trust show up? The team essentially ignored the CEO's directive and started to talk about how they were going to work around it. That was a form of fighting back and was based on Level 2 thinking as well.

We all know that once a person loses trust, it is very difficult to rebuild it. And we also know that without trust it is very difficult for a leader to influence people to take action. Very simply, without trust a leader cannot lead.

The Leader's Paradigm

In coaching women leaders in technology, I have discovered that one of the most difficult things for leaders to learn is to value our role as leaders. This is especially true for people working in highly technical fields that rely on a strong knowledge base. When we start our careers in technology and for the first 10 to 15 years, we are patted on the back and given promotions based on our technical knowledge or perhaps our understanding of process, and of course, on what work we successfully complete.

As a leader, the paradigm for how we work and how we bring value to the organization shifts. We are expected to step away from the details and be the visionary, the encourager, the lead guide or perhaps the servant leader.

For many people, not just women, that paradigm shift can leave us feeling confused about our roles. We may feel like impostors, as though our work is no longer as valuable and, by deduction, that we are not as valuable. Or we may feel as though without the details we can't control what is going on, and that can be a very scary place for a leader. It is a natural tendency to want to rush back into the details where it feels safe. As good as that feels initially, for a leader, that spells disaster. How does this entire scenario relate to Level 2 thinking?

As a leader, do you ever feel like it is a struggle to get people to get things done? When you are struggling, you are in Level 2 thinking. The feeling of struggle is a sign that you fear that your needs won't be met, especially your financial needs. Your security feels threatened.

Do you ever feel a need to control the details in order to be certain that the job will get done? Controlling behavior comes from Level 2 thinking. The need to control the details is generally an indicator that you are focused more on what others are doing wrong or might do wrong than on seeing what they are doing well.

Do you ever feel like you need to *decide for your team*? That is Level 2 thinking. The need to rule over a team is a sign that you don't trust the people on your team to make good decisions or take action that will move the business forward and meet your needs.

The bottom line on all these is a lack of creating buy in and trust with your team, not having them involved from the beginning with the objectives and expectations. When we don't involve people in our vision, then we don't know if we can trust them to do what is needed to be successful. It leaves us fearful of whether our needs will be met. What is created is a struggle that causes us to want to control and micromanage or manipulate our people and projects. We push people to get things done. We become frustrated and even angry when we feel that we might not have control over a situation. We may get sarcastic or "bitchy."

What we get in return is pushback, resentment and more fighting. I'm not saying that people are yelling or fist fighting. In fact, what you may encounter are the blank faces of people who have put up a wall of resentment against what feels like to them as disrespect or aggression.

The bottom line is: When we are struggling with a situation and trying to control it by managing the details, we may be thinking Level 2 thoughts that cause repercussions that are not what we want in our life.

But what if another person we are working with is the primary person doing the fighting and we are simply responding in kind? How do we get out of the fighter's ring or stop the circling of negative energy?

The path of least resistance

A number of years ago I was leading a system implementation for a national retailer. The retailer's executive sponsor for the project was constantly picking out minor concerns and blowing them all out of proportion, demanding more and more details.

My response was to pull together the information he asked me to gather. Every time I brought him information, he demanded more. It felt like I was being bullied. There seemed to be nothing I or anyone else could do to shift his attitude towards me and the team. Every week for months on end it was the same story. For me, it was a struggle to keep up with all the work that I felt he was unnecessarily placing on me and my team.

Even though I wasn't overtly arguing with him, I could feel my resentment growing and the tension between us was real. We weren't yelling, but the fight was on. He was going to demand what he wanted and I wasn't going to let him think I wasn't good enough to lead the team.

Luckily, during this time I had a coach who asked me to consider what else might be going on for the sponsor that could be causing him to be so unreasonably demanding. Was it true that he was angry because he didn't think that I was good enough to lead the project?

In doing a little undercover work, I discovered that he had been previously downsized and was most likely worried about his job security. His family was angry at him for moving them to a place that they hated. And, last but not least, his boss and he didn't get along. It was common to be waiting to speak to one of them and hear them yelling at each other behind closed doors.

Then my coach asked me to consider how I was responding to him. Slowly I became aware that I was reacting from my need to be accepted and valued. In my subconscious, I believed that if someone was angry that it must be my fault and I just needed to *try harder*. There's that word "hard" again.

My reaction to him made me the perfect target for him to let out his frustrations. Every time I responded by bringing him more information, it just fueled the fire. In truth, I was so concerned about my own feelings that I couldn't hear that he simply needed a safe place to vent his frustrations.

How do I know this is true? A few weeks after discovering

that I was adding to the problem, I had the perfect opportunity to change my response to him. We were in a team meeting, and he started to berate me in front of the entire team. But instead of trying to fix the situation he was talking about, I sat quietly listening until he ran out of steam. Then, without saying anything, I was able to continue on with the meeting.

After the meeting one of the team members came up to me and asked, "What was that all about?" I was able to honestly say, "He is having a rough time right now and just needed to vent."

The best part is that the aggravated demands stopped. Why? When I stopped pushing back, the opposing force had an opportunity to be released. I had found the path of least resistance. Six months later, this same person handed two new contracts to me for an additional year of work for my team. Who would have expected that to happen?

Bottom line: Just because we aren't overtly fighting doesn't mean we aren't pushing back and creating unnecessary problems for ourselves. Pushing back can take many forms and can look to ourselves and to others like we are just doing our job. It may even be something as simple as an eye roll or a sigh when we don't agree with something someone says during a meeting, and that may feel like a put down to the other person.

Please note that just because my examples were with men doesn't mean that the same thing doesn't happen with women. In truth, we all want the same thing and that is to have our needs met.

In most cases, we can't fix the other person's underlying concerns, nor should we try. What we can do is to discover how we are pushing back, stop the pushback, and allow the tensions to be released so that a very different relationship can emerge. In other words, we can think differently about the situation.

Anger in the workplace

Something that we haven't explored yet is what happens when it seems appropriate to get angry about someone's work or a situation that is causing problems. Do you think that it is safe, as women, to express our anger?

Personally, I have seen more men than women overtly express anger at work, and to a certain extent I think that it is culturally more acceptable for men to express their anger. Many women have been taught that it isn't "nice" to show our anger, and it's possible that men have bought into that stereotype as well.

The truth is that almost everyone expresses anger at some point on the job. However, in my experience, it's not anger in and of itself that is unacceptable, but instead it's the difference in the way most men and women use anger that creates an impression that it is not safe for women to express anger at work.

Here are a couple of differences that I have noticed about the way men and women generally use anger.

• Men's anger tends to be louder, more boisterous, and primarily a way to let off steam and create some energy. (Think of a bunch of boys punching and knocking each other around in fun.)

• Women tend to be quieter in their anger and to use sarcasm or what might be labeled as being bitchy as a way to express their anger. Sometimes women cry as a way to express their anger.

• Men tend to use their anger to raise energy around a situation and to trigger solutions and get past their fears as fast as possible. Their anger generally results in movement, not necessarily productive movement, but movement nevertheless.

Fighting Your Way to the Top

- Women tend to use anger as a way to work through their feelings about a situation. Since processing feelings generally takes longer, it may appear that women wallow more in their anger and their use of anger may frustrate the men who are in a hurry to come up with a solution as quickly as possible.

Women's anger also tends to be aimed more personally at another person rather than at the situation. That personal anger builds fear, which leads to pushback. In my personal experience, it has been OK to express anger at work as long as in some way I acknowledged that I was not upset at a person but was upset at a situation and followed up quickly with a strategy or requested ideas from others that would improve the situation. In my experience, as long as anger was used as the inspiration for making a situation better versus a way to simply complain or process feelings, then anger has been generally accepted.

I say generally accepted because there are some people (men and women) who don't process anger well. Some people can't get past the expression of anger to be able to hear the concern that is triggering the anger. Anger puts them into a tailspin or they may go off on their own anger binge.

Of course, the effect of anger also depends on how verbally abusive people become when they express their anger. Yelling, screaming or verbally bashing people over the head doesn't appear to work well for men or women. There may be some short-term results, but in the long term it causes a lack of trust, and no matter what the gender, it is also a prime trigger for employee turnover or being let go.

It is important to note that the type of anger that is expressed is not necessarily relegated to one gender or the other. I have seen two men, a company CEO and CFO, be fired by a board of directors because all they did was complain, yell and blame each other, and neither of them ever came up with a solution that would resolve the negative situation.

On the other hand, once upon a time I remember a very late night on a tough project where another woman and I got into a yelling match. I am sure it wasn't comfortable for anyone to overhear us, and I wouldn't suggest this as a particularly good use of communication. But it did release some tension, and we were able to quickly move forward.

In my experience, it's not about whether it is acceptable for a woman to express her anger at work. It's about whether our anger (man or woman) inspires positive forward movement or slows progress and creates a toxic environment.

Beating a Dead Horse

Level 2 thinking can feel exactly like beating a dead horse or being beaten down. Before we move onto another level of energy, it seems worthwhile to consider how Level 1 and Level 2 thinking affects not only our mental and emotional health but also our physical health. Here is a little bit about the physiology of Level 1 and Level 2 thinking.

Each one of the levels of thought is associated with an intensity level of either negative or positive thought. Level 1 and 2 thinking are associated with negative or catabolic thought, which in turn is associated with 32 chemicals or hormones, such as cortisol or adrenaline.

These chemicals are meant to be used by our bodies for good purposes. For instance, if we are in a jungle being chased by a lion or are about to be in a car accident and want to avoid it, then adrenaline and the 31 other hormones or chemicals are triggered for release into our blood stream in order to help us fight, flight or freeze for our safety. As we run from the lion, these chemicals create the energy we need in order to flee from danger. In the instance of a pending car accident, they help to shut down our left brain which allows us to make split-second decisions without having to think through each move, thus hopefully avoiding an accident. These chemicals can have a positive impact on our lives in certain situations.

However, in today's society we are rarely in situations where we need to run from a lion and hopefully we are seldom in situations where we might be in an accident. That being said, the stress, overwhelm, anger, frustration or resentment that we experience causes our bodies to react as though we were being chased by a lion or about to be in an accident. Our bodies are flooded with the same 32 chemicals in order to protect us. On the surface, that would seem to be a positive physical reaction.

The problem is that in today's world, when we are in a stressful circumstance, it isn't generally associated with a situation where we would need to run. Running or other vigorous movement is what releases those chemicals from our bodies. In most current work environments, we don't move vigorously and the chemicals don't leave our body. You might have been aware of this happening when you had to deliver a critical proposal or give a presentation to a large audience or defend yourself with your boss. You may have had an adrenaline rush that gave you the energy to keep going, but since you weren't moving, you might have found yourself feeling a bit sick to your stomach (ulcers anyone?), getting a tight throat, or not remembering what you wanted to say.

Catabolic chemicals work by breaking down parts of our body in order to release the energy we need to take action. As a one-off event, these hormones are invaluable and generally don't have a long-term effect, because they gradually dissipate and our body returns to normal. However, if we are constantly stressed or frustrated (i.e., thinking Level 1 or 2 thoughts) then we are, without realizing it, constantly flooding our bodies with these hormones. The result is that the hormones gradually break our bodies down and we literally make ourselves sick.

Besides the emotional, social and success reasons, there are very good health reasons for wanting to move the energy level up to Level 3 thinking. Level 3 thinking and above are also associated with chemicals, but they are anabolic or positive hormones, such as serotonin or testosterone. These chemicals build our bodies up, make us healthier and give us more physical energy.

Up-Leveling

What does it take to move up a level into positive thinking? First and foremost, it takes becoming aware of our thoughts and then being willing to shift our thoughts to ones that will serve us better. If something isn't working for you and you are feeling angry, frustrated or resentful, then the key is to pay attention to what thoughts are going through your mind that are creating that emotion.

Below is a list of typical thoughts that I hear from my clients. As you read them, you might find yourself saying "I would never say that." And I would agree, you probably wouldn't say most of these out loud. That being said, it's the unspoken thoughts that frequently trip us up the most and rob the joy from our work. These thoughts are often so engrained that we don't normally notice them, or we think that a thought is "just the way things are" or that they are "true." Up-leveling your thoughts to Level 3 and above will have a huge impact on your peace of mind and the joy you get from your work.

Here is the sample Level 2 thoughts list. My suggestion is that you read it out loud. If you agree with the statement or a statement doesn't feel good, it probably means that it is worth paying attention to for you. As with Level 1, take the thought that triggers you and use it as a basis for working through the Magic Formula in chapter three.

Level 2 Thoughts

- Some days I really hate going to work.
- Trying to balance my work and home life is really hard.
- Some people are just born lucky.
- I hate writing proposals / staying late at work / getting extra work dumped on me.
- If that guy pushes me one more time, I think I'll explode.
- I have to be very careful about what I say and do, because it's a dog-eat-dog world out there.
- I need to make sure that I cover my ass in this case or I could lose out.
- This company / world has really gone to the dogs.
- The competition is tough / brutal / dishonest.
- My boss doesn't give a $%^&* about me. All s/he cares about is how s/he can use me.
- It takes a ton of energy to put together even one email. Just one wrong word and I could be in hot water.
- Everyone in this company is out for themselves.
- You can try getting information from that team / boss / client, but don't expect any real help.
- You would think that just once they could get it right.
- What an idiot. A monkey could do a better job.
- If you had done your job, we wouldn't be in this situation.
- I have to watch my team every step of the way if we expect to be successful.
- I am pissed.
- I thought this job was going to be better, but it is just the

same situation all over again. It's so disappointing.
- I keep giving them more and more information, and they are never satisfied.
- No question in my mind, s/he's wrong.
- Do I have to do everything by myself around here?
- If s/he screws me out of this project / promotion, I'm going to make sure they hear about it.
- I'm going to find a way to make them pay for that remark.
- I am so tired of having to constantly keep after people to get things done.
- It is really tough trying to get ahead in this economy.
- There are only so many opportunities and if you want to get ahead, you have to practically kill yourself working.
- The only thing that really counts in the work world is what you can achieve.
- I am so sick and tired of pushing boulders up mountains by myself. Who do they think I am? SuperWoman?

Chapter 6

Living in the Yin and Yang

In the last two chapters, we looked at one level of thinking at a time. However, in this chapter I think it is important to combine Level 3 and Level 4 thinking, because at their very basic level they represent masculine and feminine thinking. Taking a look at how men and women typically think differently may help us to recognize some of the biggest traps that both genders fall into when it comes to leadership.

Kate at Level 3

Do you remember Kate, the woman who wasn't getting paid on time by her referral resource? Kate knew she needed to let go of her frustration (Level 2 thinking), because it was affecting her work and her health. We talked about what she had done in the past to get paid. She said that she had made a 2-hour round trip to their office, plus spent time waiting around so she could get a check. It seemed disrespectful to Kate that they wouldn't pay her promptly, and it seemed like a waste of time to have to drive to their office just to get a check.

As we talked, Kate realized that she was actually wasting more time and energy working around the problems the situation was causing than she would spend if she drove up and picked up the check. In the end, she decided that what she needed to do was to build a three-hour time period into her calendar every week where she would drive to her referral source, engage them in person and get paid. In other words, Kate created a strategy for getting paid. Strategy is what Level 3 thinking is all about.

Level 3 thinking is called the Strategist.

- **The primary thought of the Strategist is: I win, and if you win too, that's OK.**
- The emotion is one of being in control of our environment.
- The action is that we use a strategy to get our needs met.
- The advantage for people who have a lot of Level 3 **Strategist** energy is that they are usually very upbeat, aggressive, and get-it-done type of people. A lot of sales people have large amounts of Level 3 thinking. Traditionally, men have been trained to work and lead from Level 3 energy.
- The disadvantage with the Level 3 thinking can be understood by the primary thought, which is: "I Win, and IF you win also, that's OK." This says that as I create my strategies to protect myself or get my needs met, I may or may not take your needs into consideration.

At the beginning of describing the different levels of thought, I wrote that every level has advantages and disadvantages. It occurred to me that the best way to understand Levels 3 and 4 is if we are able to recognize both sides of each level. It is important that you, the reader, recognize that you are not wrong if you think like one of these levels. At the same time, in order to be our best selves, to be leaders that can more easily influence people, it helps to know where the traps or barriers are hidden within each level.

Level 3 Advantages and Disadvantages

Advantage: People tend to be positive and productive. They know how to "play the game" in order to win. This makes many people feel safe.

Disadvantage: Focus tends to be on short-term goals that meet immediate needs. That means that long-term problems may not be addressed and may turn into fires needing to be constantly put out.

Advantage: Level 3 people forgive people easily. They don't take things personally and can move forward quickly when a situation goes awry because of a mistake someone made.
Disadvantage: A Level 3 thought might be to forgive a person because "they don't know any better." In other words, they rationalize away problems rather than facing them head on. Rationalizing takes care of the situation for the moment, but long-term it can have the effect of wearing a shoe with a rock in it. We may learn to walk in a way to avoid the rock digging into our foot, but that can cause other problems that are generally more painful and more difficult to fix.

Advantage: There is quick movement to solve problems, to let go of the past in order to move ahead and get needs met. In my experience, this is the Level 3 thinker's greatest strength. It allows people to feel safe, because they recognize that their basic needs are being met.
Disadvantage: The tendency is to gloss over concerns, to avoid conflict, to not ask for directions or to lie or manipulate to cover any perceived weakness for fear of looking "not good enough" and possibly losing their job. However, other people often see through to the weakness and may lose confidence in that person.

Advantage: You can count on the Level 3 person to get things done and to do it in a way that is upbeat and productive. They are the first person to step up with a strategy when there is a problem, and they will work long and hard to be able to solve it as soon as possible – IF it will meet their needs.

Disadvantage: They can be so focused on solving the problem at hand or moving an agenda forward in order to get their own needs met that they don't consider how their actions may be affecting other people. Other people may sense that the Level 3 thinker doesn't care about them, and that creates a loss of trust which over time can lower productivity.

There is one last disadvantage that is important to note. If a Level 3 thinker doesn't include other people in their strategies, they don't know whether they can trust the other people to do what is required in order for the Strategist's needs to be met. This is when Level 3 thinkers start to feel a need to control the situation, watchdog their team or micromanage. That robs them of a lot of time and energy and often keeps them up at night. When we start to feel a need to control people or manipulate situations, then we have slid back down the slippery slope to Level 2 thinking or controlling. Sometimes we may refer to these people as "control freaks." Micromanaging is exhausting and time wasting for both the Level 3 thinker and the people on the receiving end.

Locked Door Metaphor

Consider Level 3 thinking in terms of the locked door metaphor. What you need is waiting on the other side of the locked door. What you will experience is that Level 3 people rarely if ever get flummoxed or at least not on the surface. They are the first people to come up with a solution for how to open the door. Level 3 thinkers tend to be very good at controlling their emotions and working logically. They know where to find the key, and if they don't know, they will come up with another strategy to get their needs met – which may or may not include unlocking that particular door.

The disadvantage is that it can be so important for Level 3 thinkers to stay in control that if they don't have an immediate answer, they might not admit they don't know. They may hide behind what sounds like a "logical reason" and try to manipulate someone else into working on opening the door. Or they may decide to go down an entirely different path, losing time in the process even when they are already close to success.

The advantage is that one way or the other, they will find a way to get their needs met without having to push against the door or break it down. And if someone accidently locked the door, they will let it go and may give a rationalization like: "They just didn't realize we would need to get through the door."

Level 3 thinking can be so focused on opening the door and getting their own needs met that they may not notice that other people need to get through the door as well, and without thinking about it, shut the door in their faces. If someone comes through the door with them, that is OK, but they wouldn't necessarily go out of their way to hold the door open for them.

This is how a Level 3 thinks, feels and takes action. What is it like to think at Level 4?

Level 4 is often referred to as the Collaborator.

Level 4 is the exact opposite of Level 3. If the majority of men are trained to think and work at Level 3 **Strategist,** who do you think are primarily trained to work at Level 4 **Collaborator?** That's right – women.

- **The primary thought of the Collaborator is: "You win, and IF I win too, that's OK."**
- The emotion is caring and compassion.
- The actions are to move other people forward towards their goals with the expectation that as others are supported to move

forward, we will move forward with them.
- The advantage is a high level of trust. They are the best at caring for others. Many people working in service industries, such as nursing and teaching, have a lot of Level 4 **Collaborator** thinking.
- The disadvantage for Level 4 energy is that if a **Collaborator** continues to move others forward or to give and give over and over and doesn't get their own needs met, they may become stressed or overwhelmed and drop back into Level 1 **Victim** energy or they may become frustrated, which is Level 2 **Fighter** energy.

Kate at Level 4

Kate's strategy was to block out time to drive up and pick up her check. That was Level 3 strategic thinking. However, after getting to her referral source's office, she sometimes found that people were busy and her check wasn't ready. Instead of saying anything, she made the assumption that she needed to be patient and to care about their needs. She did get her check in the end, but her tendency to take care of other people's needs before her own would sometimes end up eating up an entire day that she had intended to use for other purposes. If it went too long, she would end up leaving, feeling like a victim of circumstances (Level 1) or frustrated (Level 2) and then have to start all over again. Kate finally had enough and decided her business was strong enough and she was valuable enough to disassociate herself from the referral source. Her source was shocked and couldn't understand why Kate would walk away from good referrals.

It is very common in technology when women become overwhelmed or frustrated that they end up walking away from the situation. Research shows that 56% of women working in technology leave the industry between years 15 to 20. The question that is bubbling up right now is whether they are leaving for a better career or if they are leaving because they are Level 4 thinkers who have given everything they could and find that their basic needs are still not being met. As with every level, Level 4 thinking has its advantages and disadvantages.

Level 4 Advantages and Disadvantages

Advantage: People with Level 4 thinking are often found in middle management roles, because they are very good at nurturing their team and bringing them up the ranks.
Disadvantage: It is common for a Level 4 thinker to get stuck in middle management, because they are very good at serving others. Upper management may see them as not promotable, because they don't think strategically.

Advantage: People trust Level 4 thinkers, because they know that they will always take the other person's needs into consideration before taking action.
Disadvantage: Level 3 thinkers (Strategists) tend to see Level 4 (Collaborators) thinkers as weak. Sometimes a Level 4 is referred to as a nurturer, because it can feel to a strategist a bit like having an overprotective parent at work.

Advantage: Collaborators become known for their ability to build morale in the workplace, because they take into account other people's ideas and concerns.
Disadvantage: Collaboration can be confused with consensus. In other words, sometimes Level 4 thinkers will insist on getting everyone's viewpoint before moving forward to come up with a solution. This can actually backfire on a Level 4 thinker, if

the employees become fearful that a solution is not moving fast enough and that they might lose their jobs.

Advantage: If a person needs training and support, then the Level 4 person can be counted on to be there for them. It is common to find Level 4 people working in human resources or training departments of large corporations.
Disadvantage: In a problem situation, Level 4 people tend to think about how any solution will affect the employees. Level 3 people want to fix the situation *now* and may find it painful or personally threatening to have to "waste time" taking other people's needs into consideration. Level 4 opinions may be rejected by Level 3 leaders if their solution will take too much time.

Advantage: Solutions which include the needs of all employees tend to be more long-term solutions and to create a work environment that avoids constantly needing to put out fires. This type of thinking tends to create a more stable financial environment.
Disadvantage: In highly volatile situations, it may be necessary to make a quick, strategic move in order to avoid an immediate financial disaster. Level 4 people may block a quick decision by insisting on gaining consensus before moving forward.

The Door Metaphor – Level 4

The **Collaborator**'s natural instinct is to take care of others before they take care of themselves. If a door is locked and what is needed to survive is on the other side of that door, then their focus is on making sure that everyone else gets through the door. Their thought is that if everyone makes it through the doorway, then of course, they will naturally go with the department or team or company to the other side.

Living in the Yin and Yang

However, that is not what happens in most companies where there is a lot of competition. They may spend a great deal of time instructing others on how to unlock the door. They may talk with a number of people to make sure that they are using a method that allows everyone to feel that they can safely get through the door to the other side and that everyone can enjoy the riches they find there.

Meanwhile, the Level 3 thinker (Strategist) with their get-it-done now attitude, will be already walking through the door. It can be very confusing and frustrating to a Level 4 thinker to find herself standing on the wrong side of the door while everyone else is enjoying the riches. This is common in companies where strategic initiatives are valued over people skills or the focus is on short-term goals rather than long-term growth.

The Level 4 thinker may not understand or may feel hurt if a person that they trained or mentored shuts the door in their face. They may give up trying to help or walk away from an opportunity without ever realizing what happened.

Bumping Heads

Can you see where men and women might bump heads and why women, especially women working in male-dominated industries, might not get promoted as easily? Can you see that, even though we may want the very same things – such as to be valued or recognized for our work, to have financial stability or freedom, or to have a purpose with our work – there are often very big differences in how we think and take action on those desires. Those differences are for the most part split by masculine/feminine or yin/yang.

Sandy Soto, VP-Executive Talent Acquisition at HSNi, spoke at the 2015 Women in Leadership Symposium sponsored by the Florida Diversity Council. Here are a few of the ways that she has frequently heard women express themselves differently from men during the interview process, which may prevent a woman from being hired.

- If a woman sees a job description and cannot fulfill 95% of the requirements, women will express that they don't have all the qualifications – that is, if they even apply for the job. On the other hand, if men have even close to 70% of the qualifications, they will not only apply for the job but will come prepared to argue for and/or promote their case. In other words, a man will have in mind a strategy that will help him develop the skills he needs to succeed even if he doesn't have the skills at present. A woman on the other hand is more focused on how she can help people, and if she doesn't know something then how can she be helpful?
- If a man has an idea, he will tend to state it in the affirmative, such as, "We can do XYZ to solve the problem." He will state his idea or opinion as though it were the best idea. If it is turned down, he will shrug it off and go on to the next idea. Women tend to express their ideas as a question. For instance, "What do you think of this idea?" To women, this may seem like a collaborative approach, but with Level 3 thinkers, it has the effect of making women sound unsure.
- If a woman is turned down for a job, her general reaction is to ask for feedback. She wants to make sure that she is going to be able to *please* whoever hires her. If a man is turned down, he will tend to argue as to why he is the right person for the job. His focus is more on strategizing to get the job.

Masculine Versus Feminine

You may be thinking at this point that the masculine approach is better than the feminine approach, and in some cases that could be true, especially if you are working in a competitive environment.

On the other hand, there are many advantages to the feminine approach. Think for instance about how we grow our teams.

Taking a lesson from child psychology, studies show that when we appreciate a child for their growth or for what they contributed, they are more likely to move forward with enthusiasm than if we congratulate them for the results. Women are more likely to praise for contribution, because that feels more collaborative or like praising a child for sharing. Men tend to praise for results, because winning is where they are focused. This is a very subtle difference in how we express our appreciation that can make a huge difference in a person or team's response and their future results.

Let's say your team just completed a major portion of a project. You get the team together, perhaps have a wrap party, and you praise the team for getting the project done on time and on budget. The praise probably feels good at the moment. And therein lays the concern.

Praising results doesn't last, because it is focused on something that they already accomplished. Have you ever wished for something like a car, and then once you owned it, the excitement only lasted for a short time before it started to represent just another payment or additional time that you had to spend maintaining it? The same thing can happen when we praise work results. It feels good and then it's over. Some people will start looking towards the next project, but at the same time may be thinking more about what it is going to cost them to do the next project than what good is in store for them.

By contrast, let's say that you talk to the team and point out what each of them contributed to the success. For instance, you pick out John and you thank him for a specific piece of design work that helped the team to complete the project on time and point out how this will be valuable to him and the company in the future. Now John knows exactly where he can focus his efforts, where he is valuable and where he can effectively contribute on the next project. He is more likely to be eager to start the next project, because he knows how he can be successful.

Overall, men tend to get better short-term results but create more anxiety in the workplace. Women tend to create a better work environment but it may take longer to get the same results.

Bottom Line

Bottom line: There are advantages and disadvantages to both Level 3 and Level 4 thinking. The question then becomes how do we know what to think in order to be successful?

In 2011, Stanford University did a study of highly successful women. They discovered that women who were able to consciously switch between what is seen as primarily a masculine style of leadership (Level 3 Strategist) and a feminine style of leadership (Level 4 Collaborator) not only were able to surpass the other women in their field but they were also surpassing the men.

What that says on the surface is that to be successful, both women and men need to be able to easily move between the **Strategist** and the **Collaborator** ways of thinking.

Personally, I think there is a problem with that theory. A **Strategist** is unlikely to take on a **Collaborator** role at work, because it may be perceived as weak. And a **Collaborator** is less likely to take on a **Strategist** role, because it may seem self-serving.

Many women, especially women working in male-dominated industries, often work at taking on a more masculine approach in their leadership role. They become more competitive, hardline, no-nonsense, strategic. To a certain extent, that can work for women. However, a couple of things can happen that may backfire on women. One factor is that if women go overboard with the masculine role, they can be seen as unfriendly, and being likeable is a key component of anyone's success. I experienced this personally. Do you remember the "Star Trek" series with Captain Jane Way? When I realized that my team was calling me "Captain Jane's Way" behind my back, it became clear that I had gone too far towards taking on an unnatural characteristic of being too controlling or aggressive.

The other thing that happens if women take on too much of a masculine role is that it goes against the grain of a collaborator's natural self. It can become very exhausting trying to be someone we are not. This unnatural way of being, I believe, is possibly the biggest reason women leave the technology industry. I have said it before and I'll repeat it here: Women don't want to be like men. They want to be women, and if they can't be their natural feminine selves, most women – no matter how good the prospects – will eventually leave. Women may not realize what is going on. They may only realize that they are tired of being in an overly aggressive environment.

So, what is the answer? I believe that it is for all of us to move towards Level 5 thinking. However, before we do that, let me give to you a comparison of how Level 3 and Level 4 think, so we can be really clear about the differences and what would further propel us to move to Level 5 thinking.

Level 3	**Level 4**
I can make this happen.	What does everyone think we should do?
You made a big mistake on this report.	Do you see any ways that you could improve this report?

I'm sure I can convince them to see it my way.	Let's make sure we have a consensus before we move forward.
People make mistakes all the time. We have to just let that go and move on because they don't know any better.	Serving people, helping people fix their problems, is important and nothing feels better than doing so.
There isn't a hurdle that I can't overcome in some way.	Everything will work out fine if we believe it will.
If I do something that is wrong, it's generally better just not to say anything and move on. What I can't see won't hurt me.	I make mistakes like everyone else and there is always something I can do to improve myself.
Life is what you make it. You can create a purpose and live it with the right connections.	You can value your life by what you do for humanity, to make the world a better place.
The past is not important. Let's live for today.	The past is not important. Let's live and love.
I'm in control of my life and I know how to play the game and make my life work.	There is no need to control anything, but I do like it when my life is working.

Step 3
WiseWoman Leadership

Chapter 7

Opportunity Knocks

Barbara had been on a job search for six months and was getting ready for an interview for a position as the marketing executive with an international medical technology company. It was an opportunity of a lifetime for her, and we were talking about how to approach the key interview with the CEO of the company. "When he asks me what I can do for the company, how can I best respond?" she asked.

We didn't need to talk about Level 1 thinking (avoid saying anything or talk around the answer) or Level 2 thinking (be defensive or abrasive), because she was already determined that this interview was going to have a positive outcome.

Level 3 thinking would mean that she would be totally talking strategy, which she thought would appeal to her interviewer but at the same time would leave out the people picture which she felt was critical to the company's success. Level 4 thinking would be more focused on the people aspect but not on the strategy. What she needed was an approach that took both Level 3 thinking and Level 4 thinking into consideration.

At that point, I asked her what outcome they both wanted for the business. She responded that they both wanted to successfully open the U.S. market.

Then I asked her what solution she had that would most likely result in meeting their common goal, and she was able to outline a solution that was both strategic and addressed the people connection.

When she interviewed, her focus was not on the problem of how to open a new market but on the solution and the opportunity for both of them. By presenting herself as part of that solution, the interviewer was quickly able to see how they could be successful. And yes, she got the offer.

Level 5 is known as the Reconciler, meaning that people with a lot of Level 5 thinking have a very high level of respect for the need for both Level 3 and Level 4 thinking. They respect the need for both strategy and collaboration, and because of this level of respect they are able to reconcile the two different ways of looking at the same situation and quickly move to a solution that will meet both needs.

This level is sometimes referred to as the level of opportunity. The reason is that when a situation isn't working, they don't see it as a problem. They only see the opportunity in the situation. Every situation is an opportunity to improve their skills, make a better widget or build a stronger relationship.

- **The primary thought at Level 5 Reconciler is: "We both win."**
- The emotion at Level 5 is calm or peace.
- The action is that we walk side by side, supporting each other so both of us get our needs met. In other words, the barriers disappear.
- Advantage: There is less blaming between working partners, work is calmer, solutions come faster.
- Disadvantage: It takes more up-front time to establish the vision and culture that will support Level 5 thinking.

There are so many advantages to Level 5 thinking. Can you imagine how much work would get done if people stopped blaming each other when situations weren't working as planned? Can you imagine how calm it would be? Wow! That isn't to say that we would always agree on everything, but when a situation did come up that wasn't working, we wouldn't waste time pointing fingers at each other, because we wouldn't see it as a problem. Instead, we would both be focused on working towards a solution to reach a common goal that would meet both of our needs.

Door Metaphor – Level 5

The door is locked and on the other side of the door is something that you both agree that you need in order to not only survive and also thrive. Before you attempt to unlock the door, you take the time to agree to key factors for getting through the door, such as: You won't break down the door but will find a solution that maintains the integrity of the door; both people will get through the door at the same time; and the riches will be split so that both parties benefit. You brainstorm a bunch of ideas and come up with what seems like the best solution. You move forward quickly. Halfway through, you discover the solution is not working because the door is too narrow for both people to get through together. Neither party wastes any time blaming the other person for what isn't working. Instead, they immediately look for an improvement that will meet their pre-determined criteria. They decide to draw a number that will determine who goes through the door first, and they agree that the first person going through the door will hold the door open for the second person.

This is a very simplistic look at what happens when people are at Level 5 thinking. As one client put it, there are no banging heads, no male/female put-downs, no leaving people behind – it simply works. There is a strong trust level. Both parties believe that the other person will follow through, because in order for either person to "win," they both have to win.

Getting the Right People on the Bus

You may have read the book *Good to Great* by Jim Collins and remember that one of his first tenets of success is to "Get the right people on the bus." One of the easiest ways to assure that you get the right people on the bus is to start with Level 5 thinking.

There is psychological evidence that opposite personalities are attract each other. For instance, an artist might be attracted to a scientist because their talents and skills are complementary to each other. However, when we are talking about levels of thinking (or energy), then like thinking/energy actually attracts like thinking/energy. For instance, have you ever walked into a conference room meeting with a large group of diverse people and noticed how they were grouped? On the edges are the Level 1 thinkers who tend to avoid interacting or getting involved because that is what feels safe. Then there is the group over on one side that is standing around complaining about the same things they complain about every day at the water cooler. Those are the Level 2 thinkers. There is the group who is deep into conversation about what might come up in the meeting and how they will handle any concerns. These are the Level 3 thinkers. And there is the group who is running around making sure that everyone has the right notes and knows what to do during the meeting. Those are the Level 4 thinkers. Finally, there is the group that is simply enjoying the moment, having a conversation about an idea they are planning to put forth in the meeting, enjoying each other's company. Those are the Level 5 thinkers.

What you want to notice is that if it is true that people who have similar perspectives or think alike are attracted to each other naturally, then if we are leading from Level 5 thinking of the **Reconciler,** we would naturally attract clients and employees at that level – and that is a really easy way to get the right people on the bus.

Kate at Level 5

Let's say that Kate, the person who wasn't getting paid on time had been thinking at Level 5 and her referral resource had also been a Level 5 thinker. In that case, Kate and her referral source would have sat down early on and set expectations that would have met both of their needs. What might that have looked like? Maybe they would have decided together that in order to meet both of their needs, they needed to schedule a fixed time for a weekly meeting to discuss their caseload in person, decide who would handle each case and talk through any concerns that had come up regarding their clients. They could have agreed on expectations for each person, including when payments would be made and how and what would be the consequences of either party not following through on their part of the agreement. When a situation wasn't working with a client, the focus would be on how to resolve the situation as quickly and effectively as possible. It would not have been on Kate or her referral resource alone to resolve the concern. Kate would not have had to worry about whether she was doing a good job or not, because there would have been an open discussion. And she wouldn't have worried about getting paid, because they would both be in agreement as to how that would be handled. Instead of looking for what was going wrong, they would look for what was going right, see the value in each other's contributions and celebrate their mutual successes.

True Win-Win (Moving from Level 3 to Level 5)

It is interesting that many people will say to me, "Jane, I do think Win-Win." Oftentimes when I am coaching a leader and things get tough, however, they discover that what they were actually thinking was: "I win, and if you win too, that's ok," or "You win, and if I win also, that's OK." What comes into play at the Level 5 thinking is that both people win or no one wins.

"Competition is the thief of joy." -Theodore Roosevelt

Competition or Enthusiasm

This brings us to a discussion about competition relative to Level 5 thinking. A client called me one day feeling really blue. She had worked hard for six months on a proposal, and that day her company had learned that their proposal had lost. It meant not only a big let-down personally, but it was also going to be tough to figure out how to keep the company solvent. They had been counting on that project.

She said that the competition had been fierce. Just trying to make sure that they had done everything they could to beat out their competition had made the process stressful and at times overwhelming. Have you ever been there?

Our discussion had me thinking about competition in general. Is it good or is it bad? Is it really a necessary component of doing business? Is it possible to go beyond that level of thinking? Is it possible to run a successful business without competing?

Educators tell us that competition can be good for students, because it can motivate them to stay alert, to notice more and to try harder. Business people say that it helps to create more efficient, better and cheaper products and services and to build a stronger economy. Some psychologists say that competition points out our strengths and weaknesses, and accentuating our strengths allows us to succeed more quickly and easily.

On the other hand, there are some definite disadvantages to competition. Competition can cause us to focus on the wrong thing – like focusing on the competition instead of our client. Competition can create stress that shuts down our capacity to think clearly and come up with creative solutions. And completion can suck the joy right out of our work and stop us from wanting to take the risks that would allow us to be successful.

Here's a thought. What if we exchanged competition for enthusiasm? Competition exists whenever it is expected that you or the other person will win or lose (Levels 1-4). Enthusiasm is a hallmark of Level 5 thinking.

Before we consider what this exchange could do, it would be helpful to define the word enthusiasm. The origin of the word is from Latin and Greek and is a variant of the word entheos, meaning "to have a god within" or "possessed by a god." In today's world, it has come to mean "possession of the mind by an interest or a pursuit."

What is interesting to me is the difference in where the drive or impetus comes from when we look at competition versus enthusiasm. When we use competition as our driver, we are relying on something outside of us, something over which we have no control. When we use enthusiasm as our driver, the energy is coming from within ourselves.

Let's look more closely at the example of working on a proposal. If you are competing, then you spend time making sure that you don't miss anything that your competitors might include in their proposals. You might research your competition's websites or you may talk with people who have worked with your competitors in the past.

What happens to our mindset if we find out that our competition is a newbie in the field? Do we stop working as hard on getting our proposal right, because we believe that we can easily beat them? Does our presentation unconsciously get a little sloppier or is it perhaps not as well thought out in terms of what the client needs? Do we miss side conversations from the client that could be helpful in our proposal, because we think we have it wrapped up? Is it possible that the newbie has something so incredible that they surprise us and end up blowing us away?

What if we find out our competition is the biggest and the best in the field? Do we subconsciously give up, because we believe we can't beat them? Or do we go into a frenzy trying to figure out how to outdo them and end up putting all our attention on what the competition is doing and losing track of the client's needs? Do we work ourselves so hard that we are exhausted and start making mistakes? Do we wake up in the middle of the night worried about what is going to happen if we lose?

What happens if we exchange competition for enthusiasm? At this level of thinking (Level 5), what is driving us? Is it the thought of creating something really incredible? Is it the desire to make a huge difference for our client? Are we focused on both parties winning? If we do wake up in the middle of the night, is it because we suddenly have this amazing idea that we know is going to allow our product or service to be exactly what the client needs or better? Are we so enthused that we can't sleep and get up and start working on it right away? Do we put every ounce of ourselves into the proposal because we can hardly wait to see our product or service come to fruition and make a difference for our client?

Competition (Levels 1-4) or Enthusiasm (Level 5)? What's your take on these two drivers? How would you like to spend your career?

Moving from Level 4 to Level 5

Many of the women I coach are very caring and compassionate Level 4 thinkers, and I am very grateful to be able to work with them. One of the wonderful results of having Level 4 characteristics is that we tend to trust people when we know that they care about us. And we all know that trust in relationships is a primary key to being able to influence people to commit to us and take action. What leader wouldn't want to be trusted by their team

The downside of caring and compassion is women's tendency to take care of everyone else's needs and not our own. I know that this is not a new concern. There are many articles about making sure we eat right, sleep right and get plenty of exercise. And there is plenty of recognition as well for the need to set boundaries that keep us from taking on too much work or being in a relationship with someone who drains our energy.

What we may not always recognize are the times when, as a leader, we take on responsibility for work that really belongs to someone else. Let's look at an example of where this might happen.

A client is trying to determine how to organize her team in order to be the most effective. She asks whether she should create two teams that specialize in different areas of work or cross-train everyone for all the jobs. She is concerned that if she breaks the team down into specialized areas, they will be very proficient in their areas but might not see the whole picture and make a wrong assumption or do something that won't work. On the other hand, if she cross-trains everyone, then they may not have deep enough skills in either area to be highly effective.

We brainstorm some ideas and she decides that she will break the team into specialized units. In her kickoff meeting, in addition to articulating the goals, deadlines, responsibilities and expectations, she will also give everyone a high-level overview of the entire project. She thinks this is a good plan, because it will give everyone an understanding of where to go and who to talk to if they have any questions about the direction of their work.

She also suggests that in addition to daily "standup meetings" where she checks on their progress, she will add a mid-project meeting to address any cross-team concerns. Again, a good idea in that she can use this time to ask questions and make sure that everyone is on the same track.

At this point I stop the brainstorming and asked my client a question. "Who is doing all the work to make this plan successful?"

Yes, you've got it. It's the leader. The leader is doing the training. The leader is preparing an overview for the kickoff meeting. The leader is holding meetings to make sure that people are working in sync. The leader is checking up on their progress. In other words, the leader is taking all the responsibility for the teams being successful. Is it any wonder that some days her stress level is off the charts?

This is exactly the type of situation where women tend to do work that appears at first to be our responsibility, but in reality is the responsibility of the entire team. We take all the responsibility on ourselves and then wonder, "Why are we exhausted, stressed or overwhelmed with our work?"

What about the team? What is their role in making sure that they and the project are successful? Are they expected to just sit at their desk and "do their job," or do they have a larger responsibility to the team and the project?

Next question: How do we get the team to take on a greater share of the responsibility for the project's success while at the same time keeping the leader abreast of what is happening?

For a few minutes we discuss options, such as making a point to publicly praise people who, when they are unsure about a course of action, make an effort to take on responsibility for reaching out to other team members. "Of course," my client says, "keeping track of who is taking on this responsibility will mean more work for me." Finally, my client says quite honestly, "I don't know. I'll have to think about it."

At this point I put on my mentor hat and propose an option. I ask, "What do you think will happen if…"

- You sit down with your team at the start of the project and together you create a very clear vision and expectations for a successful project that the team can buy into fully.
- You talk through the potential risks of someone making a mistake because they only understood their particular specialized area of work.
- You ask the team to come up with a process or method for identifying and mitigating those risks.
- Together you determine what level of work and the type of interactions that will be acceptable and what will not be acceptable, and how the team wants to handle a situation that goes off course.

My client's response is, "Yes! That could really work. They would be creating the rules or the process and would be more engaged in making it happen. And I wouldn't have to watchdog the project as much." Still wearing my mentor hat, I re-emphasize that the key will be to make sure that the vision and expectations set for the team and the project are clear enough that they can stay on target.

This is Level 5 thinking. It is leadership where we create a clear vision and expectations that people can genuinely buy in to and then handoff the "how to" to the team. It means engaging our teams and putting the responsibility as well as the authority for the success of the project in the hands of the team. It means giving our team the same level of trust to get the job done that they give to us as leaders.

When it gets personal

Marianne Williamson, in her book *Return to Love*, tells a story about a man she once dated. After several dates, he mentions that he has one ticket to an event that they are both interested in attending. Marianne tells him that he should go to the event and that she will stay home and watch the event on TV. Afterward he can come over and they can share their experiences.

The event is over, it's midnight and her date has not shown up. She waits up until 3 a.m., oscillating between being angry and worrying that something happened to him. The next day she expects him to call, but the call never comes in. She wonders if he met someone else, did he use this as an excuse to back away from their relationship, or is he just inconsiderate?

For several days, she fumes. Then she decides it is a waste of time. She tells herself that she forgives him and is letting him go. She repeats this thought to herself every day for a couple of weeks. Finally, one day she realizes that she really is over him. Then, of course, he calls. "Hey, Marianne, I miss you. How about going on a date tonight?"

Her response is what I really want you to pay attention to now. She says, "I really like you, and if you want to meet up for lunch sometime just as friends that would be fun. But I don't want to go on a date with you, not because I don't like you as a person but because your expectations and my expectations for dating are not the same."

What has this story to do with work? Most women, especially women whose thinking is predominately that of the Level 4 Collaborator, take situations much more personally than men, and this isn't just on the dating scene. It's at work as well.

Taking things personally can cause women to hang on too long to a job, hoping that it will get better. It may cause a woman to worry about something that went wrong and play it over and over in her head, wondering what she did wrong and leaving her exhausted. It may create a barrier between her and the men in the office who just want to fix the problem and move on. Taking things personally can stop her from setting reasonable boundaries. It can prevent her from being promoted, because she dwells so long on a problem and doesn't take quick action to change the situation.

In my experience, the biggest problem with taking too personal of a perspective on a situation gone wrong is that neither we nor anyone we are involved with in the situation truly gets their needs meet.

Let's look at a couple of work examples.

Say our boss is "on our case" for not making the numbers every month. As women, our tendency is to immediately start thinking that we did something wrong. Our brain immediately senses danger and puts us in "fight, flight or freeze" syndrome. When that happens, 32 chemicals or hormones are released into our bodies to help us deal with the danger. One of the chemicals causes us to narrow our focus. This is very important when we are in danger and looking for a safe hiding spot. However, when we are in a situation where we are trying to come up with options for meeting our numbers, it's a disaster! What if we hadn't taken the situation personally but simply looked at the situation as something not going the way we intended? What if our mind was open to seeing different opportunities to solve the situation?

Here's another situation to consider. Let's say that the economy takes a downturn and the company we work for has to lay off some people whose skills were important to the business, and the business is suffering. The boss asks us to pick up the missing tasks. We don't say no because we take the situation personally. We don't say no even if we don't have the skills to be effective in that role. If we take the situation personally, we may spend a long time trying to "fix" the problem, even when we logically know this isn't possible. We may avoid confronting the real problems in the situation. We may hang on to a job too long. We end up stressed, frustrated and exhausted, and wondering why.

Please don't think that I am promoting that we should stop caring about other people. Women tend to think that if we don't take something personally, we are being cold or unfeeling. But notice what Marianne said to her date. She liked him. Her decision didn't have anything to do with whether he was a good person or not. It was just that their dating expectations were different.

When we take things too personally, we really are doing a disservice not only to ourselves but also to everyone else involved in the situation. In fact, when we take things too personally, who are we really thinking about? Yes, we are thinking about ourselves. And when we are focused on ourselves, it is easy to slip into being defensive about even small things that aren't working the way we would like them to work and that is Level 2 thinking.

Consider what would happen if we looked at negative situations for what they really are: an opportunity to change something for the better, to find a better solution, to help someone really solve a problem instead of putting off the inevitable. This is Level 5 thinking.

Disadvantages to Level 5 thinking

With so many advantages, it may be difficult to anticipate what could be the disadvantage of Level 5 thinking.

First of all, in the beginning it takes more time to establish a Level 5 environment. It takes time to include people in developing a common vision and to create the parameters that will point to solutions and that will meet everyone's needs.

However, once the vision, common goals and parameters are established, leaders who think as a Level 5 **Reconciler** generally find that everything moves along much more quickly and easily because the barriers have disappeared. They're not wasting time on in-fighting (Level 2) or having to watchdog people (Level 3) or constantly nudging them forward (Level 4). At Level 5, the toxic work environment that we see in many companies shifts to a healthier environment.

Another disadvantage is that if you are a Level 5 leader and your client or people on your team are not in tune with Level 5 thinking, they may simply not get it. Then you may need to consciously respond with approaches or tactics from other levels of thinking in order to meet them where they are. This does not mean that you drop back to the lower levels of thinking. It means that you recognize where the other person is coming from and respond to them in words and actions that they can understand. It is a conscious choice to use the tactics from the different levels versus reacting from those different levels of thought without an awareness of how we are reacting.

Here are some examples.

- We may bring on board a very technically competent employee who needs to get up to speed. As a Level 5 thinker, we would make a mental evaluation of the other person's needs, recognize that the person is not up to speed and consciously make a choice to spend extra time supporting the new employee. The difference between using Level 4 tactics and thinking at Level 4 is that a true Level 4 thinker automatically responds to all situations from a collaborative or nurturing point of view. It doesn't require an evaluation or decision on the part of a Level 4 person to offer support. The Level 4 person will approach a situation from Level 4 thinking even when it isn't necessary or may be detrimental to the situation.

• We may have a team of Level 3 hot-shot sales people who are in a hurry to get out the door, and we have to jump in with a **Strategy** in order to capture their attention and direct them to become aware of how their actions are affecting the company as a whole.

• We may have some talented team members who have lived so long in frustration that they don't recognize that there are other ways to approach their work and life. At times, you may find that you need to consciously take on the role of the **Fighter** in order for them to hear you, and from there work to move them up the levels of thought.

• And there may be times, hopefully not often, when you consciously need to take on the role of the **Victim** and avoid a situation temporarily, such as when a client or employee goes into a rage or you get included in an argument that isn't going anywhere.

Hopefully by now you can understand what makes me say that in order to be a WiseWoman (and WiseMan) Leader, we need to reach for Level 5 thinking. Below are some typical thoughts I have heard that represent Level 5 thinking that can give you some ideas about how you can start moving in that direction.

Level 5 Thoughts

- Business is great. Everywhere I look there are opportunities for growth.
- I'm curious as to what you think about this situation and what would bring you to that conclusion.
- Everyone on our team has unique skills that they bring to the table and participate fully. That makes my job easy.
- When it seems like life is taking a bad turn, I know to stop and consider how I am thinking about the situation and to turn my thinking around so that I can move forward again quickly.
- I am working on the most fascinating project. It's fun to think about all the different ways we can improve our client's business.
- We stayed up half the night brainstorming about ways to approach the gooey layer that will make it easier for our employees to navigate the new system.
- Let's check to make sure that we hit all the major parameters for this project and that what we are coming up with will meet the key needs of the entire team.
- This month I not only applied for and received government certification for small business contracts, I also enrolled in a cyber security training. It's important to me to keep growing myself.
- The client was really in a huff today. I wonder what that was all about?
- Knowing that we are making a difference in the world and that our work has purpose, makes it easy to keep going when the project hits a rough patch.
- Focusing on what is going wrong or blaming other people when a situation goes awry is a waste of effort. Better to spend our time brainstorming solutions.

Chapter 8

Comparing 5 Levels of Thinking

A wonderful client of mine frequently asks for an A/B comparison in order to fully grasp a concept that I have shared with her. This chapter is for her and everyone else who may be feeling a bit overloaded with information and needs a different way to focus in on how the levels of thinking can affect different situations. Hopefully it will also serve as a quick reference guide for when you find yourself in a situation that isn't working for you and need some guidance on how your thinking differently might cause a shift in the circumstance.

To review, these are the first 5 levels of thought that we see most often in the work place. They include:

- Level 1 – The Victim
- Level 2 – The Fighter
- Level 3 – The Strategist
- Level 4 – The Collaborator
- Level 5 – The Reconciler

Here is a way that might help you hold these levels in your mind. Let's go back to the example of the door that we used to demonstrate each level and compare them.

Imagine that you are starving. You walk up to a building and you can see through the window that there is a table set with all kinds of wonderful food and people sitting around the table eating. However, the door is shut and locked and you don't have an invitation to the table. What do you do?

Level 1 (Victim): The victim may make the assumption that the food isn't for her. She may watch people going in through the door but avoid trying to open the door. She turns away, resigned to being hungry.

Level 2 (Fighter): The fighter might bang on the door or push her shoulder into it to try and break through. She may even go so far as to break the door down in order to reach the food and get her needs met. It is a struggle and feels hard. People at the table don't find her actions to be acceptable. However, at least she isn't going hungry.

Level 3 (Strategist): Invited or not, the strategist will find a way to open the door and get to the food. Maybe she rides on the coattails of someone else. Maybe she comes up with something to exchange for the food. At the very least, the strategist is going to reach for the door and open it, even if they have to manipulate someone into giving them food.

Level 4 (Collaborator): The collaborator's first thought is: "If I can give them what they want, then I'll get what I want." They offer to serve everyone in exchange for food, and that works up to a point. The problem is that there are no guarantees that they will get the good food instead of the scraps or nothing at all.

Level 5 (Reconciler): The reconciler's first thought is: "What if…" The reconciler doesn't even realize that there is a problem. All they see is opportunity in any situation. What they are focused on is the table of food, not the closed door. Their assumption is that if everyone works together, they can easily open the door and everyone will get to eat.

Next Steps

Now that you have the overview of the levels, let's delve into comparing some real-life situations that will help you to see how shifting to higher levels of thought can make a difference for you.

Example 1: A team member blames you

It is about 7:30 in the evening. We would prefer to be eating dinner, but the project is behind schedule and we are all working extra hours to get it back on track.

Steve, the engineer on the project, walks into my office with a distressed look on his face and says with a bit of edge in his voice, "I think that the lead on a technology project should be an engineer."

I'm the lead on this particular project. Although I have had some experience programming and have spent years finding alternative software solutions for businesses, I am not an engineer. How can I respond to this person's comment?

Level 1: Avoid responding. I think inside my head, "He's right. I probably don't belong in this position. I 'should' know more details about the technical aspects. I should be an engineer." We walk away and I avoid the conversation.

Advantage: When people feel that they are being attacked, often the first reaction is to push back. The advantage of Level 1 thinking is that it feels self-protective and it avoids any verbal conflict.

Disadvantage: What I'm not addressing is that Steve has a problem. With my Level 1 response, the engineer's concern isn't resolved, and I am thinking that I'm not good enough.

Level 2: Frustration grows. It's nearly midnight and I'm sitting in my hotel room. I can't sleep because of this interaction. Suddenly it dawns on me that "He has a lot of nerve." Oh yes, now I'm at Level 2 thinking. The fighter has come out in me. "If I were a guy, would he have had the nerve to say that to me? How dare he! Does he think I'm a wimp just because I'm not an engineer? Who does he think he is? If I was an engineer, I wouldn't have needed to hire him to lead the technical team." Round and round go these thoughts in my head.

Advantage: I've stopped the self-pity and shifted my thinking into a place where I can potentially take some action.

Disadvantage: Nothing is getting resolved. Anger is rising. Both of us are losing sleep and the project is losing time.

Level 3: A strategic action takes form. It's 7:30 a.m. the next morning and we're back at work, and nothing has been resolved. My Level 3 strategist kicks in. I think, "He can't help it if he doesn't have an answer. He is doing the best he can with the resources he has. The client is living in the dark ages and hasn't been particularly helpful. What I need to do is call in for some additional technical support. I'll have to convince the powers that be that we are shorthanded and the engineer needs more support."

Advantage: Finally, some forward movement. With the right technical support, the engineer will be able to have someone to do the detailed research he needs to solve his concern.

Disadvantage: The engineer hasn't been consulted and he may not be comfortable with my strategy. My strategy may solve a technical problem and at the same time create a leadership problem.

Level 4: Opening the conversation. It's noon and my Level 4 thinking takes over. I invite the lead engineer to lunch to try to smooth things over. I let him know that I have found a way to fix his problem, that I've asked for another engineer to support him. To my surprise, he lashes out at me again. He says, "Do you think I am stupid, that I can't do the job? Are you trying to get rid of me?"

Advantage: I'm bringing the engineer into the loop and making an effort to keep our business relationship working so that we can move the project forward. I've avoided getting angry at him and have opened up the conversation so that he feels comfortable in the future asking for support when he needs it.
Disadvantage: Now everyone is going to know that he has a problem that he can't resolve. There is no way for him to save face. I thought I was helping him, but he sees my attempt to fix the situation as demeaning and threatening.

Level 5: Finding the opportunity. We have been through the first four levels of thinking. No one is happy or productive. What would have happened if my first reaction had been from a place of Level 5 thinking? What could that have looked like?

Level 5 thinkers would not think that there is a problem. Even though they would recognize that a specific situation isn't working, they would immediately engage the engineer in looking for the solution. The conversation could have gone something like the following.

My first step might be to acknowledge the elephant in the room by saying something like, "What I think I hear you saying is that there is a concern and you need some answers, and you wish that I could provide you with those answers. Is that a fair assumption?"

When he agrees (or corrects my assumption), then I might validate him and move the situation forward by saying something like, "I get it that there is a problem and you are frustrated because the answer isn't coming to you. What have you tried so far?"

or "What other options are available?" or "Do you know people you could talk with about your concern at a higher technical level?"

Advantage: Now that the concern is out on the table and he knows he is not in trouble for not having all the answers, we can move forward. We don't waste any time pointing fingers at each other. The door is now open to looking for the best solution in this situation.

Disadvantage: If the person who blamed you is not a level 5 thinker there may be a disconnection with your expectations.

Example 2: Your boss criticizes you

It was afternoon on the Wednesday before Thanksgiving and most people in the company were getting ready to leave early for a long weekend. Suddenly someone realized that the technical plan that was in place to support their clients over the long weekend had a big gaping hole.

A new plan was quickly developed to fill the gap. The only problem now was how to make sure that all of the employees who would be involved in the change got the message before they left that afternoon. That meant notifying hundreds of people in a very short timeframe. Many had to be convinced to delay their vacation, and some even had to change their airline tickets for later flights in order to make the necessary changes.

The woman in charge of getting the message out realized that time was of the essence and that there was no way of knowing if a person was working at their desk and would receive an email in time. She decided that the most expedient way to deal with the problem was to work with the people who were in charge of making emergency loud speaker announcements. She also had to create messages that would inspire people to agree to change their holiday plans and not leave the company or their clients in the lurch.

It worked. Employees got on board, made the changes and saved the day.

Like me, it may seem that she would have received a big pat on the back for her quick thinking. But instead, her boss found her and criticized her for using the loud speaker system, because now everyone in the company knew there was a problem. How could she respond?

Level 1: Quietly take it on the cuff. "I'm sorry. It was the best I could do in the moment."

Advantage: She most likely avoided a big confrontation. For many people, this feels like a safe answer.

Disadvantage: Notice that at Level 1 thinking it is common to hear a person say "I'm sorry," even when there is nothing to be sorry about. Constantly saying "I'm sorry" is a self-inflicted put-down, and her boss may see her as a weak link.

Level 2: Express your resentment. "I didn't have much of a choice. The team made a mistake and I had to fix it fast."

Advantage: She was able to make her voice heard and point the conversation back to what caused her to need to take these steps.

Disadvantage: Being defensive builds a wall. It's possible she just started a silent fight with her boss that could undermine her later.

Level 3: Take control of the conversation. "This was not a normal situation. The problem had to be addressed quickly or we would have lost some major players. I stand by my actions."

Advantage: This is an assertive stance that tough bosses often relate to easily.

Disadvantage: If the boss's criticism is coming out of fear of something like losing his job, it may leave him wondering if he can trust her to protect his back.

Level 4: Fix the boss's immediate concern. "You seem concerned about how it was announced. I apologize if I unintentionally caused a problem. How can I help you to do damage control?"
Advantage: The boss knows that she understands his underlying message and that she is concerned about making it right with her boss. This may release the boss's tension.
Disadvantage: She just put her boss's monkey on her back and has become an easy target to blame when other things go wrong.

Level 5: Focus on a solution. "What I think I hear you saying is that there is a gap in our internal communications because we don't have a way to alert people in a situation like this without broadcasting it to everyone and making our department look bad."

If you get a positive response, follow up with 2 questions. "What do you think we need to do immediately to do damage control?" and "What if we put together a team to think through how we can respond in the future in a way that is both timely and directed only at the people who need to hear the message? Does that work for you?"
Advantage: You put the elephant out on the table without blaming anyone and responded with a solution so that the boss does not have to be concerned going forward.
Disadvantage: Sometimes people (bosses included) are so driven by fear that they cannot move quickly to a solution way of thinking and this can be frustrating for both people.

Example 3: Resolving a major disagreement

A team of software developers were working on integrating a new system into an old financial system. About three months into the project, the leader for the development team came to my office to let me know that there was no way that they could finish the project by the end of the year. There were too many decisions that had still not been made regarding the new system. Plus, the old financial system was going to need some changes as well, in order to be able to accept the new information.

We went together to talk with the CFO about making some changes to the schedule. The CFO went ballistic. The prior week he had presented the monthly financial report to shareholders. The report included information on the system changes that were being made and how these changes were going to improve their bottom line. He had promised the stockholders that the new system would be in place by the end of the year and that (pounding on the table) was what was going to happen. No excuses! He didn't care if the developers had to work 24/7 to get it done. (Have you ever heard a statement like that? Oh, yeah.)

The leader for the development team started to get a bit hot under the collar. I thought for a second he was going to start swinging, but he managed to hold his temper and say with emphasis, "It isn't going to happen. The schedule was too tight to begin with, and you have asked for changes that were not included originally, and we need more time. Even if the team works 24/7, we won't be ready, because we still don't have final decisions on a number of changes."

At that point, I was starting to get concerned and realized that I needed to do something quickly. We had a problem. What we needed was a solution. How could I think about this situation that would help to solve this dilemma?

Level 1: Hope for the best. In other words, you could say nothing, let the two people with the concern work out a solution and avoid getting in the middle of the argument.

Advantage: If they make a decision on how to move forward and things go wrong, then you wouldn't have to take the blame. It feels safe, especially in a room where there is so much tension. It also allows you to block out the tension and just do the work that needs to get done.

Disadvantage: There is a strong possibility that either no decision will be made or that the CFO will force an answer on the engineer. This will put pressure on the engineer and his team, and potentially create resentment and put more toxins in the environment. Productivity would mostly likely go down.

Level 2: Force a decision. The project has a timeline. Some business leaders say that the best thing to do when there is a problem that needs an immediate shift in direction is to implement the change, start moving forward quickly and then adjust as needed.

Advantage: The power in this approach is that work keeps moving forward. People don't waste time arguing alternatives. In some ways, it is a little like agile programming, where you move quickly and have stopping points where you can adjust to meet the desired outcome.

Disadvantage: If time is of the essence, it can seem like forcing a decision is the fastest way to keep moving forward. However, if key people are not included in the decision and there isn't an agreement on the preferred outcome, it may cause longer delays in the middle of the project and actually slow down the project, or you may end up with a product that is less than what was expected.

Level 3: Take control of the situation. The project leader con-

Comparing 5 Levels of Thinking

vinces the CFO to bring in more technical people to work on the integration so it can be done in the timeframe that the CFO is asking for and doesn't overburden the development team or cause them to miss their deadline.

Advantage: The project can start moving forward quickly. The engineer, whether he is in complete agreement or not, knows what to do and can take action. The CFO can tell the stockholders that the project is moving forward and his personal credibility will be upheld. The engineer will have more people to work on the project, increasing the prospects of completing the project when the CFO wants it done.

Disadvantage: There simply are no guarantees. Yes, the project will move forward more quickly…or not. The engineer is now going to need to find the additional people, bring them up to speed and integrate them into the project. Sometimes that works, sometimes it doesn't. Meanwhile, the project is over budget and the pressure for meeting the budget ends up on the back of the project leader instead of with the CFO and the engineer.

Level 4: Make a collaborative decision. Collaborators generally want to make sure that everyone who will be affected by a decision will have their specific needs met. Generally that means checking in with the heads of different departments or holding meetings to announce any changes and get feedback.

Advantage: When the needs of everyone are taken into consideration, then in most cases morale is raised. Higher morale commonly equates to higher productivity. Higher productivity equals higher return on investment, better products, and lower turnover.

Disadvantage: Collaboration is when people are on board with doing what needs to get done. Sometimes people confuse collaboration with consensus, needing to get everyone's approval before moving forward. Needing consensus can slow progress down to a crawl; the project may lose all momentum and even stall out.

Level 5: Look for the opportunity. The reconciler is always looking for the way forward that will meet the needs of both parties. I asked the CFO what it is he needed, and he said, "I need good numbers coming from the new system that we can show to the stockholders at the end of the year." Then I asked the engineer what he needed, and he said that he needed time to integrate the systems so that they get good numbers the first time and don't have to go back and do a lot of rework. Where is the opportunity? They both are looking for good numbers from the new system by the end of the year.

Advantage: Once the common goal was recognized, it was easy to determine that we could delay the integration and use a hybrid version of parallel processing to provide the answers that the CFO needed to give the stockholders as well as give the development team the time to do their best work. This decision also had an unexpected benefit in that the accounting department had been concerned that they would have to go through an audit with two different systems, and now their job would be easier.

Disadvantage: Not every CFO is going to be as astute and willing to make adjustments to the plan. Furthermore, people working on the project may not be able to mentally switch gears as quickly as is needed to accommodate the change. It may take some extra time and coaching on the part of the project manager to get people on board and moving forward.

Try it!

Now that you have some examples as a guide, you may want to take a situation that is happening in your office and write out how you might respond from each level of thought. It may help you to go to the end of each chapter on the different levels and look for other typical responses.

Start by outlining the situation. Then write out how you would normally respond in that situation. Note the advantages and disadvantages of responding in that way. If you find that your normal response isn't working for you, then experiment with other options. The more you do this, the more your thinking will shift and the easier it will be for you to respond to situations in a way that is the most constructive for you as a leader.

One last thought before we move on to Level 6 and Level 7. Sometimes when we respond in a certain way, it doesn't work out for us. What I often see is that people will then take the situation home with them and lose sleep over it. My suggestion is that if how you respond doesn't work right away, don't beat yourself up. After all, that is Level 2 thinking. Instead, be a Level 5 thinker and look for the opportunity in every situation.

Chapter 9

Beyond the Ordinary

Usually when I talk with a group of people about WiseWoman Leadership, I stop at Level 5, because in general, that is as high a level of thinking as the best leaders attain on a regular basis. If, as a leader, you create an environment where people go peacefully about their work and are highly productive every day, I would say you have done an incredible job, wouldn't you? That is what it is like when you have created a Level 5 environment.

Level 6 and 7 thinking is beyond the ordinary. Only a handful of people live at Level 6 or 7 thinking most of their lives. As one man said to me, "I can't imagine being there all the time. You wouldn't be able to relate to most people." He has a point.

However, there is always one person who asks, "But what about level 6 and 7 thinking?" I delight at their question and this is what I say to them.

Level 6 is like being in the flow of life. Have you ever had one of those days when you drove down the road and all the lights turned green and when you got into the parking lot, the spot right near the door to the building opened up in front of you? That is what it is like to be at Level 6 thinking. It is the same feeling that an athlete describes as being in the flow, where time seems to stop and everything feels free and easy.

Level 7 is what I describe as the "guru" level of thinking. It's that moment when you are standing in the shower or taking a walk on the beach or meditating and, without knowing how or why, a brilliant solution is downloaded into your mind. You are able to see a situation on many levels and you know exactly what to do that will serve the situation and the people in that situation in the best manner. Level 7 is the level of pure genius.

Wanting to be in the flow, having our life feel free and easy, downloading genius ideas is appealing to most people. If this is you, then let's take a little closer look at what it means to progress through these next two levels.

Level 6: The Level of Flow

- **The primary thought of a person who is at Level 6, Flow is: "We all win."**
- The emotion is one of permanent joy.
- The action is the feeling of being in the flow. It is associated with a lessoning of judgment of self and others.
- The advantage for people who have a lot of Level 6 **Flow** energy is that they have a sense of connection with everyone and everything in their lives.
- The disadvantage with the Level 6 thinking is that while you may be in the flow, others may not be, and it may appear to others that you are simply lucky or that you have your head in the clouds.

Level 7: The Level of Pure Genius

- **The primary thought of a person who has a lot of Level 7, Genius, thought or energy is: "There is no win or lose."** Similar thoughts that go with this primary thought include: There is no right or wrong, no good or bad.
- The key emotion is one of pure passion for all of life.
- The action is the ability to see life from all directions, to not judge it and to live life fearlessly.
- The leadership advantage is that a person with a lot of Level 7 energy is able to see situations from many points of view, not judging any one point of view but being able to recognize what

is the best solution for the present situation. It is pure genius.
- The disadvantage is that a person with a lot of Level 7 energy may seem in some way disconnected from other people because of their ability to see life from so many points of view. To many people, Level 7 just doesn't seem realistic.

Your Key to Living and Leading with Ease, Grace and Integrity

The most important thing for you to understand about all the levels is that you already have the capacity within you to be at whatever level you choose. It may appear some days that you are a caged bird. But you already have the key to the cage, and all it takes is for you to make the firm decision to unlock the door and let yourself out.

The key to your particular "cage" is what philosophers and psychologists and religions refer to as: letting go of the ego, surrendering, stopping the noise, closing the book on the stories we tell ourselves, dying to self and rebirth, letting go of self-deception, and seeing our physical selves as temporary and recognizing the spiritual world as the real, permanent world.

Science, particularly the study of quantum physics, is catching up with what people have been observing since the beginning of time. Who we are in the physical world and how we experience the rest of the world is a product of how we think, as that makes up the patterns and filters in our mind. Who we are and how we see the world changes when we change our thoughts and beliefs.

In order to be in the flow of a Level 6 thinker or to have the genius ideas of a Level 7 thinker, we have to be willing to discover and let go of the patterns that don't serve us. If it is your desire to move past Level 5 thinking and discover what it is like to live in the flow, there are four areas of thought associated with growth into Level 6 and 7 thinking.

Non-Judgment: Both in my personal experience and in my experience as a coach, non-judgment is the area that seems to take the most time to develop for most people, and at the same time it has the most power to change our lives.

In order to be in a state of non-judgment, we have to accept that there is no right or wrong, no good or bad, no positive and negative. When I say this to people, I often get looks like, "Are you crazy? Of course, there is right and wrong."

Without going into a lengthy discussion (this topic is a book in and of itself), I will simply say that non-judgment is tied into letting go of our ego. Ego is our physical and mental self. Ego sees the separateness between our physical selves, and we perceive that we are different and judge one person as being better than or inferior to another. In letting go of our ego, we see everything as one. Spiritually, this has been a guiding principle in most major religions. Science now recognizes that at the lowest molecular level, we and everything on this earth are of the same material, which is energy.

When we are able to let go of judgment, we feel very joyful and full of passion for life, no matter what is going on around us. We love and value the people we live and work with, and they love and value us.

- **Intuition:** Intuition will always take you further than knowledge. When we trust our intuition and make decisions from this space, then our life just flows along. The lights all turn green, genius ideas come to us, and life feels easy. Have you ever spent a lot of time analyzing a situation and then suddenly an idea came to you that was in opposition to the analysis, and yet you knew intuitively that it was the best answer for the situation?

Most people will claim that they have intuitive abilities and that would be true, as every person is innately intuitive. The key to a powerful intuition is to actually trust it and use it on a regular basis. When we trust our intuition, it is a sign that we also trust ourselves and other people. If we flip that idea, the way to develop your intuition is to begin by learning to trust yourself and in turn to trust others.

- **Purpose:** If you don't have a lot of energy or enthusiasm for life, chances are that you are not living purposely. Many people live purposely in some areas, but not so much in other areas. If you aren't living purposely, it will affect your ability to be successful in your work.

When we talked about leaders who have a lot of Level 1 energy, we said it was often associated with not being fully committed to their work. Not being fully committed is a reflection of not living purposely. If you sense that your energy is low and that you aren't 100% committed to your work, then living purposely will have a huge impact on you.

- **Allowing:** When we are in pain, most people wish that it would just go away. Perhaps we try to ignore it or push it down. Perhaps we try to diminish our pain with food, alcohol or any number of abusive actions. This never works, because it isn't eliminating the pain – it's only hiding it. The instant something happens that triggers a memory of the pain, we are right back where we started.

The only way to permanently release pain is to face it, to "allow" it to come to the surface of our attention. What does that mean? It means that we see our pain. We notice where the feelings of pain are coming from and how it is affecting us, the people we interact with and our work. Then we make a decision on how we will let our pain affect us going forward.

Now that you know the four areas where shifting your thinking can lead to Level 6 and 7 living, let's do an exercise that will help you to take the first step in that direction.

Who are you?
(The first step to non-judgment or letting go of your ego)

Humor author Dave Barry frequently writes about the difference between men and women. One of my favorites scenarios is when he describes the way we differ when we look in the mirror in the morning. If a man has 8 hairs on the top of his head, he will spread them out on his head like a big spider and then look in the mirror, puff out his chest and pump his fist while shouting out, "Yeah, Yeah, Yeah!"

On the other hand, a woman will look at herself in the mirror, find a pimple the size of a pinhead on her face and shriek, "I've got a pimple!" as though the world is coming to an end. She may even cry. Then she'll spend the rest of the day asking her friends if they notice anything wrong.

OK, this is probably exaggerated. But seriously, aren't we funny creatures? We (women) have a tiny pimple or a new wrinkle on our face and it can cause us stress that lasts all day and longer. Yes, it is a little stressor, but in some ways, it can actually cause more stress than the thought of losing our job or the death of a beloved. If we have a big trauma, most of us will eventually find a way to work through it. However, the tiny pimple sets off that mean little voice in our head about how we aren't beautiful enough or good enough or smart enough or valuable enough or loveable enough. That little voice is there, day in and day out, nagging us. It never lets up or goes away. We carry it with us wherever we go. And the accumulative stress from that little voice – that Level 1 thinking voice – is enough to break us down. How we think about ourselves is such a habit that most of us aren't even aware that we are talking negatively to ourselves.

I have to ask: If you had a friend that talked about you the way you talk about yourself in your head, would they still be your friend? Of course not! In a flash, we would walk away from them. And yet we carry that inner voice with us everywhere we go and allow it to determine who we are in the world.

To make this more real, let's do an exercise together. If you don't have one nearby, stop and get a pencil and blank piece of paper. If you are reading this in a place where you can't get to paper and pen, then draw a picture in your mind.

Here is what we are going to do. Take your pencil and create three columns. In the far-left column, draw a stick picture of yourself going to work. You don't need to be an artist and you don't have to show it to anyone else. This is simply a representation of how you look when you go to work or perhaps out to lunch with friends. This is what I looked like in my stick drawing. If you want you can draw your picture next to mine.

Underneath your drawing write 3 characteristics of yourself going to work. I wrote:
- looking smart
- pulled together
- upbeat

What are your thoughts about yourself going to work? You can write them down here or on a separate piece of paper, whatever works better for you.

_____

_____

_____

OK, now that you have a picture of yourself going to work, move to the middle column of your piece of paper. Draw a stick figure of yourself first thing in the morning, naked and looking at yourself in the mirror. Did I hear you snickering or rolling your eyes? LOL. It's OK, everyone has this reaction. Just go ahead and draw. No one needs to see the drawing but you.

Here's my stick figure of me naked. You can draw yours next to mine if you want.

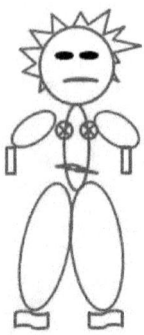

Now write down 3 characteristics of yourself standing naked in the mirror. I wrote: Heavy thighs, bad hair and getting older.

_____

_____

_____

Now imagine what your inner voice is saying to you. Mine says things like:
- Hey, I don't look too bad today.
- Oh, come on, you are getting so fat. Look at those thighs.
- Well, nobody should care about that. I have a great brain and I contribute a lot to the company.
- I wonder if I'll will ever be thin like Mary?
- I wonder if anyone will notice the pimple on my face. It's really not that big.
- Who am I kidding? I look like a teenager with that pimple. They'll probably think I have the brain of a teenager.

This may not be your voice, but I guarantee you have a voice in your head that is saying something to you almost constantly, whether it's positive or negative. Even the guy who spread the eight hairs out on his head like a spider is saying something to himself. His voice may be more like:
- If I comb my hair this way, no one will notice that I'm getting older and going bald.
- Who am I kidding? They probably already have my exit strategy all planned out.
- Well, if I act like I'm full of energy, I'll get by for now.
- How am I going to support my family if I get laid off?
- That woman who sighed during my presentation, she must think I'm losing it.

Let me ask you another question. If your boss or a colleague talked to you the way you talk to yourself, would you go to them for advice? Of course not! The voice in our head is all over the place. One minute it's building us up and the next minute it's tearing us down. And yet we listen to that voice battling inside of us all the time. That's our Level 2 voice. With our thoughts, we create our own stories and our own frustration and anger! Nothing outside of us causes the amount of stress we have as much as that voice inside of us.

The same thing happens with the business relationships in our lives. Let's say you have a boss, and one morning s/he doesn't follow their normal habit of stopping by your office to check in. The voice in your head starts up:

- I wonder why s/he didn't stop by my office?
- S/He is such a jerk for not calling.
- What's wrong with me?
- Oh my god, maybe s/he's going to fire me.
- I can feel it coming.
- I shouldn't have spoken my opinion so boldly in that meeting.
- Well if s/he doesn't think enough of me to overlook a bit of aggression, then I don't want to work for him/her.

The voice in your head goes on and on. And then the phone rings. S/He got tied up in a meeting. S/He says, "I apologize that I didn't stop by to catch up with you this morning. Everything got so crazy and time got away from me. Do you have 10 minutes now to fill me in on what's going on?"

We often have no idea what is really going on, yet we have this running commentary that is creating stress and fear and frustration or a need to control or a need to fix everyone's problems. And it isn't just sometimes. The voice in our head, whether we are paying attention to it or not, is talking to us almost all the time.

Do you now recognize that we really only have one major problem in life? It isn't what is happening outside of us. It's the voice inside our heads that won't be quiet.

And it isn't just the voice of when we are naked in front of the mirror. It's also the voice at work that says we have to dress a certain way, act a certain way, work a certain way and if we don't, then we aren't good enough. If we don't have a great idea that day or someone ignores our idea, then we aren't smart enough or knowledgeable enough. If we don't make a sale, then we aren't assertive enough or we aren't friendly enough, or we're too aggressive or talk too much.

It doesn't matter if we have a bad hair day or a bad idea day, that little nagging voice in our head beats us down. I'm not saying that we can't improve skills. I am just talking about the voice that keeps all of us from reaching Level 6 and 7 thinking on a regular basis.

If you aren't the voice or the pattern in your head, then who are you really?

Who are you really?

There is one more step in the exercise that we have been doing together. This one may take a little more thought. But it's worth it, because it will show you a great deal about who you are in just a few minutes of thinking.

Think about a person or perhaps several people whom you admire or love or appreciate. These can be people who are alive or dead. They can be real or fictional. They can be famous or they can be your next-door neighbor or family member. Your relationship to this person is not important.

If it helps you to focus, sit back in your chair, relax and take a few long breaths. If you want to, you can close your eyes and imagine these people.

When you are ready, write down on your paper or on the lines below 3 characteristics that you admire most about this person or persons.

_____

_____

_____

This is what you need to know about this exercise: The characteristics you wrote down are actually who you are when you let go of your ego. Let me say that again. The characteristics of the people you admire are actually your characteristics when you quiet the mean little voice in your head. Psychologically, the good that we see in other people are projections of our own true characteristics. Stop here a minute and let that sink in.

Some of you may be thinking, but I'm not always that person who is compassionate. I'm not at all courageous. It is possible that some of your characteristics are underdeveloped or hidden behind a false mask that we think society expects from us. Maybe you act tough but are really gentle. Maybe you act afraid but are actually courageous. No matter how developed (or not developed), the characteristics you wrote above (and probably a number more) are who you really are as a person.

You may be thinking: But what about the characteristics that I don't admire in others. Are those me as well? No, they are not you, but they do point to your fears about who you might be. We say things like, "Well, I don't want to be a bitchy person like that woman." What we are really saying is that I am afraid I could be a bitchy person.

The qualities that we love in the people we most admire are a reflection of who we truly are as a being, and the qualities we don't admire are not us, but only who we fear we could be.

What I hope for you

As we come to the end of this book, I hope that you will be encouraged to let go of your ego and the self-deceptions that you have built up about yourselves, and fully discover who you are and lead from this place within you.

Below are two very simple exercises that you can do each morning to help you let go of your ego and see your true self. You don't need to take an hour a day meditating. You can do these exercises in about 2 minutes or less in the morning. And you can repeat them quickly whenever you start to forget.

Exercise #1 – Who are you?

1. Take a piece of paper and create three columns.

2. Repeat the exercise you just went through putting the person that is dressed to go to work on the left, the person naked in front of the mirror in the center. List the characteristics under each picture that you listed when you first did this exercise.

3. In the right-hand column, list the characteristics of the people you most admire, love or appreciate. Above this list create a symbol or picture that represents these characteristics. It can be anything that reminds you of your true nature.

4. Put the picture up in a place where you can see it each morning. Your bathroom mirror is a handy place. Or perhaps next to your computer.

5. Every morning, look at each of the pictures for a few seconds, starting at the left and moving to the right.

Repeat as many times as you like, always starting from the left and ending on the column where you described your best characteristics. Gradually your subconscious mind will start to replace the negative thoughts about who you are with the knowledge of who you truly are. Watch for how you start to respond differently to your work. Notice how other people start to respond differently to you.

Exercise #2 – Looking into your own eyes

This is possibly the simplest and at the same time one of the most powerful exercises I have ever used to support myself and my clients in letting go of our respective egos and discovering who we truly are within.

1. Put your face near a mirror. Look into your eyes in the mirror.

2. While you look into your eyes say to yourself, "I love you."

3. Sometimes people find that in the beginning, it is difficult even to look into their own eyes. If that is true for you, simply go that far. When you get comfortable looking into your eyes, then add the phrase, "I love you."

What if...???

What would happen if we always saw ourselves as the person that we just described? What if, instead of trying to live up to society's expectations, we saw our internal beauty? What if, instead of berating ourselves for some little physical or mental difference, we noticed the positive energy of our being? What if, when we looked into our own eyes and said "I love you," we sensed a truth about that statement?

How would our life be different if, when we went off to work each day, we saw ourselves as the characteristics that we love about the people we most admire and that reflect our best self? How much more joyful would our life be?

This is where it starts, your journey to being a WiseWoman Leader. This is your key to leading with ease, grace and integrity.

The Feminine Advantage

Chapter 10

A New Perspective

Women have an untapped advantage in the workplace.

Let me say that again: Women have a an untapped in the workplace.

You may be thinking, "Have you lost your mind? What advantage? Most businesses are built on the male model of leadership. Most businesses are run by men. Men dump on women all the time at work."

OK, I admit that in some ways, you are right. If you look strictly at the current status of business, it would appear that men have the advantage in the workplace.

However, I believe that the main reason men still have all the advantage is because women generally don't realize the power that we hold and so we don't use it. (And I'm not talking about sex, in case that is what you are thinking.☺)

Where our power as women comes from is relative to thought and energy. Remember that Einstein said that everything is energy. Even our thoughts are energy. What you may or may not have recognized yet is that at each shift upward in our thinking, we also increase our energy level. Most men are naturally Level 3 thinkers and most women are naturally Level 4 thinkers. From a thought and energy perspective, most women naturally think at a higher level.

And...and this is a huge "and"...the higher our level of thought or energy, the better leaders we become and the easier life becomes.

(*Let me stop here a minute because some of you may be thinking that this is starting to sound a bit like "man bashing" and that is not the intention. Both men and women have important characteristics that they bring to the table. Please read on to understand this concept fully.)*

The monster mistake that women tend to make is thinking that in order to be successful, they need to fall in line with the way men think. But that is impossible. We can behave or take on masculine tactics (i.e., Level 3 Strategist), making our lives feel more unnatural and difficult , but we can't reverse our thinking.

For example, when you were a child maybe you thought there was a real person named Santa Claus. Then one year someone hinted that Santa Claus might be fictitious. You started to question your parents. Eventually they admitted that Santa Claus is a symbol for generosity and joy and is not a real person. Once that new thought took hold in your mind, you never again thought of Santa Claus as a real person. You may have pretended he was real, because you wanted to not let your younger sibling know the truth just yet. Or perhaps it made it fun for you at Christmas time to pretend there was a Santa Claus. Or maybe you saw it as a wonderful way to teach your children about being generous. However, no matter how much effort you put into creating this fictitious Santa, your thinking about Santa Claus as a real or fictitious character had permanently changed.

The same is true for all our thoughts. Once we become aware of a different perspective, it is a permanent shift. If our natural tendency as women is to think as a Level 4 Collaborator, what happens in the workplace when we take on the behavior of men, i.e., take on the tactics of Level 3 thinking? Several things take place.

First of all, it adds a lot of work to our plate and can be exhausting, because it isn't natural to our way of thinking. We have to think through how to respond to each situation or conversation instead of reacting naturally.

Secondly, since we are attempting to go downward on the level of thought and energy, we lose momentum. It feels like being a race car and then having to add extra pollution controls. It may fix the pollution concern, but it also reduces the overall speed and value of the car.

And thirdly, because being at Level 3 isn't who we are naturally, to the person who is at Level 3 it feels like we "just don't get it." It can feel to the Level 3 person that we are wearing a mask or trying too hard to fit in or are unfriendly.

From where we are now, it may seem that women are stuck between a rock and a hard place. If we act naturally, like women (Level 4), we may be seen by Level 3 people (mostly men) as weak. If we take on the role of Level 3, then we may be rejected as being tough or not trustworthy. If this is true, then where is our advantage?

Our advantage (drum roll please) is that it is easier, in fact much, much easier, for a Level 4 thinker to move up to Level 5 thinking than it is for a Level 3 thinker.

For people who are predominately Level 3 thinkers, the biggest block to becoming Level 5 thinkers is the learning curve that is necessary in order for them to focus externally rather than internally. You may remember that the primary thought of the Level 3 person is "I win and if you win also, that's OK". In other words, a Level 3 person isn't particularly interested in what the other people on the team need, as long as their needs are being met. In order to think "Win-Win" and to be effective Level 5 leaders, it is critical to consider the needs of other people on the team. For Level 4 people who are naturally nurturing, looking outward is normal behavior and it is a shorter up-leveling of thought to reach Level 5 thinking.

You may remember the study by Stanford University that said that the women who were able to switch back and forth between strategy (Level 3) and collaboration (Level 4) were not only more successful than other women but were also more successful than their male counterparts. However, it is a lot of work to have to think about when to use each level.

What if, instead of trying to tactically switch back and forth between levels, women made use of their feminine advantage and made the jump to Level 5 thinking? What would that do? It would mean that we would naturally, without extra work or effort, incorporate the best aspects of both Level 3 and Level 4. Our integrity would be fully intact. Our work would feel much easier. And, instead of pushing our way to the top like SuperWoman with a briefcase of kryptonite, we would gracefully rise in the ranks as true WiseWomen.

What could that look like in the real world? Here is an example. Stan was head of the IT department. When his boss brought me in to manage a big project, he was not happy for many reasons. First of all, even though he was up to his eyeballs just keeping the department running, he felt that he should be in charge of the project. Second, I am a woman and he did not take well to a woman moving in on his territory. This was his job, his department and he was going to make it clear that I was a short-timer. Finally (and to me this is the biggest reason for him being disgruntled with my presence), the environment we were working in had a huge trust issue. Blaming was the game of the day. If someone made a mistake, it was not uncommon for someone to "tattle" to upper management or to denigrate another department in order to protect their department.

From the very beginning, Stan was on the defensive. He played all kinds of control games, such as suddenly not being available when we were holding a team meeting or claiming that he had not been given information when it had been discussed in a meeting, or claiming he had never received a critical email. Worst of all, if a mistake was made, he would blast it out over the entire company without giving anyone an opportunity to correct it first.

It took extra time to carefully work around him and support him when he needed something from our team. Very gradually, I built some trust with him and it started to get a little better.

Several months into the project, we were running a test and discovered that in an earlier project some of the electrical setup had been done incorrectly. As we dug into the situation, it turned out that this was a problem at more than half of the locations where we were intending to do a new install. When I went to discuss it with him and talk through how to resolve it, he practically screamed, "Who knows about this? I suppose you went and rattled the CFO's cage about this!"

As I listened to him, I recognized his reaction as normal in this company. Getting him to think Level 5 was going to take a while. What occurred to me was to respond with a Level 2 tactic and match his anger. I shouted, "What? Do you think I'm an idiot? Of course, I didn't tell the CFO. We don't need him breathing down our necks. This is our problem to fix."

I was quiet for a minute while he absorbed my answer (and for me to chill and gather my thoughts). He wasn't used to having someone yell back and at the same time support him.

First, I came back with Level 4, "Stan, I am here to support you, not to get you in some kind of trouble."

Then I came back with Level 5. "What I want to talk to you about is coming up with a strategy so we can move forward with the current project and at the same time fix the electrical problems. Do you agree?"

We did come up with a solution. However, this wasn't the end of the blame game. It continued for several more months. And there were occasional little "tests." One day, Stan came into the team room and complained loudly about someone on the team talking behind his back to the CEO about another problem we had uncovered. Stan was livid. He went on for several minutes about not being able to trust the people on this team. The "offender" was standing in the team room and heard his outburst. This opened up an incredible opportunity to move the team towards Level 5 thinking. We talked about working as a team and having each other's backs and how, if we didn't work together, we were going to miss the project deadline and all of us, every single one of us, was in jeopardy of losing our jobs. And we all want to win, right?

A funny thing happened about a week later. At least once a week I would go out early in the morning and buy some donuts and bring them in for the team. It was a small thing to do for a team that was working as hard as this one was working. Stan walked by in the morning and saw us munching on our donuts and laughing, but he had always walked by as though he didn't notice. That morning, a week or so after his latest outburst, he stopped in the doorway and said, "Hey, I see you have donuts."

Internally I was smiling and saying "Yes – got him!" Externally we invited him in for a donut. From that moment on he was working with us, giving us what we needed to succeed, eating donuts with us and laughing. And succeed we did, with flying colors.

How does this story demonstrate the feminine advantage?

Notice that Stan was mostly reacting from Level 2 and Level 3 thinking. That means he was focused on either having someone else lose (the normal toxic environment) or on himself winning (controlling his environment). Thinking about someone else winning (Level 4) wasn't even on his radar. However, if he was ever going to get to Level 5 thinking (win-win), he would first have to be open to being concerned for the rest of his team. In other words, he had to take two steps to get to Level 5 thinking.

On the other hand, my natural bent is as a collaborator. That year of the project I had been working with a coach on getting my thinking to reach a Level 5 in more situations. It was easier for me than for Stan to take that step, because I was already focused on how to help the other person succeed. It was one step instead of two steps for me to get to "We both win." In addition, because most times I was able to think at Level 5 when working with Stan, it was easier for me to respond with tactics from each of the lower levels without sinking into to reacting or lowering my energy.

It's true that until that year I had thought that thinking like a woman was a disadvantage. Like many women, I had spent a lot of effort learning to respond at Level 3, i.e., being more strategic. And it didn't hurt me career-wise to learn to use strategy more effectively. However, as mentioned earlier, even though it helped me to "get things done," it didn't make me particularly likeable and work, as much as I loved the actual work, always felt like a struggle.

Being Level 4 never felt like an advantage until I realized that not only did it feel easier to work from Level 4 thinking because it was more true to my nature, but it was also a huge advantage from a leadership standpoint, in that I could more easily move into Level 5 thinking.

My challenge to women

In my way of thinking, this story also points out that the responsibility for changing the culture of an organization belongs to women, because most women naturally see the path to Level 5 more clearly.

Well, thanks a lot, you might be thinking. You want the women who are being rejected or pushed aside by the men in the organization to take the lead in changing the culture?

Yes, that is exactly what I hope you will do. If you think about it, does it really matter who makes life better? Wouldn't it be great to know that women were responsible for changing the business culture in a positive way? Wouldn't it be wonderful if work for everyone, women and men, was full of ease, grace and integrity?

And so, I leave you with this challenge: I challenge you to use your feminine advantage, to become Level 5 and higher thinkers, to be WiseWoman Leaders, and in so doing to lead the change we all wish to see in the world.

You already hold the key to your success. All you need to do is to use your feminine advantage to unlock the door.

Acknowledgements

We all know that it takes a village to bring up a child, and likewise it takes many people to write a book. I am grateful to all of you who have encouraged me to keep going.

Susan Hicks, my dear friend and editor, who has several times helped me to get out of a writer's block and always makes whatever I write a thousand times better.

Kimberly McClure of White Studios for pulling me out of the dark ages of design and developing an outstanding cover and book design.

Layne and Paul Cutright, for their superb relationship coaching and introduction to the concept of Radical Personal Responsibility.

Bruce Schneider, for his development of the Energy Leadership tools and the iPEC school for coaching.

Jessica Rivelli, for supporting me through her Working Women of Tampa Bay networking group.

My clients (unnamed for their protection), who have provided me with the understanding I needed to be able to write this book and the examples that make the concepts in this book real for my readers.

My Monday morning coaching group, without whom I would never have attempted much of the work I am doing today: Barbara Hardin, Charlene Pillot, Monica Roche and Lori Stephens.

The people who read my book as I was writing it and gave me critical feedback along the way: Kathryn Earle, Liz Iachello, Kelly Hamm, Leisa Rasmussen, Cecily Sharp-Whitehill and Patrick Wheeler.

Donna Spencer, for encouraging me to take my blogs and turn them into a book, and Chris Angermann, who would nudge me about the book whenever he saw me.

Last but not least, to the one person who has put up with me day in and day out as I grew into this book, my husband, Robert Barr.

www.ingramcontent.com/pod-product-compliance
Lightning Source LLC
Chambersburg PA
CBHW070619300426
44113CB00010B/1583